Donald Grant Mitchell

English Lands, Letters and Kings

Vol. 4

Donald Grant Mitchell

English Lands, Letters and Kings
Vol. 4

ISBN/EAN: 9783337817664

Printed in Europe, USA, Canada, Australia, Japan

Cover: Foto ©ninafisch / pixelio.de

More available books at **www.hansebooks.com**

ENGLISH LANDS LETTERS AND KINGS

AND KINGS

The Later Georges to Victoria

BY

DONALD G. MITCHELL

NEW YORK

Charles Scribner's Sons

MDCCCXCVII

TROW DIRECTORY
PRINTING AND BOOKBINDING COMPANY
NEW YORK

FORECAST.

—

THE printers ask if there is to be prefatory matter.

There shall be no excuses, nor any defensive explanations : and I shall only give here such forecast of this little book as may serve as a reminder, and appetizer, for the kindly acquaintances I meet once more; and further serve as an illustrative *menu,* for the benefit of those newer and more critical friends who browse tentatively at the tables of the booksellers.

This volume—the fourth in its series of English Lands and Letters — opens upon that always delightful country of hills and waters, which is known as the Lake District of England ; — where we found Wordsworth, stalking over the fells — and where we now find the maker of those heavy

poems of *Thalaba* and *Madoc*, and of the charming
little biography of Nelson. There, too, we find
that strange creature, De Quincey, full of a
tumult of thoughts and language — out of which
comes ever and anon some penetrating utterance,
whose barb of words fixes it in the mind, and
makes it rankle. Professor Wilson is his fellow,
among the hills by Elleray — as strenuous, and
weightier with his great bulk of Scottish manhood; the *Isle of Palms* is forgotten; but not
"Christopher in his Shooting Jacket" — stained,
and bespattered with Highland libations.

A Londoner we encounter — Crabb Robinson,
full of gossip and conventionalities; and also that
cautious, yet sometimes impassioned Scottish bard
who sang of *Hohenlinden*, and of *Gertrude of
Wyoming*. Next, we have asked readers to share
our regalement, in wandering along the Tweed
banks, and in rekindling the memories of the
verse, the home, and the chivalric stories of the
benign master of Abbotsford, for whom — whatever newer literary fashions may now claim allegiance and whatever historic *quid-nuncs* may say
in derogation — I think there are great multitudes

who will keep a warm place in their hearts and easily pardon a kindred warmth in our words.

After Dryburgh, and its pall, we have in these pages found our way to Edinboro', and have sketched the beginners, and the beginnings of that great northern quarterly, which so long dominated the realm of British book-craft, and which rallied to its ranks such men as Jeffrey and the witty Sydney Smith, and Mackintosh and the pervasive and petulant Brougham — full of power and of pyrotechnics. These great names and their quarterly organ call up comparison with that other, southern and distinctive Quarterly of Albemarle Street, which was dressed for literary battle by writers like Gifford, Croker, Southey, and Lockhart.

The Prince Regent puts in an appearance in startling waistcoats and finery — vibrating between Windsor and London; so does the bluff Sailor-King William IV. Next, Walter Savage Landor leads the drifting paragraphs of our story — a great, strong man; master of classicism, and master of language; now tender, and now virulent; never quite master of himself.

Of Leigh Hunt, and of his graceful, light-weighted, gossipy literary utterance, there is indulgent mention, with some delightful passages of verse foregathered from his many books. Of Thomas Moore, too, there is respectful and grateful — if not over-exultant — talk; yet in these swift days there be few who are tempted to tarry long in the "rosy bowers by Bendemeer."

From Moore and the brilliant fopperies of "The First Gentleman of Europe," we slip to the disorderly, but pungent and vivid essays of Hazlitt — to the orderly and stately historic labors of Hallam, closing up our chapter with the gay company who used to frequent the brilliant salon of the Lady Blessington — first in Seamore Place, and later at Gore House. There we find Bulwer, Disraeli (in his flamboyant youth - time), the elegant Count d'Orsay, and others of that trainband.

Following quickly upon these, we have asked our readers to fare with us along the old and vivid memories of Newstead Abbey — to track the master-poet of his time, through his early days of romance and marriage — through his journeyings athwart Europe, from the orange groves of Lisbon to the olives of Thessaly — from his friendship with Shelley, and life at Meillerie with its loud joys and stains — through his wild revels of Venice — his masterly verse-making — his quietudes of Ravenna (where the Guiccioli shone) — through his passionate zeal for Greece, and his last days at Missolonghi, with one brief glimpse of his final resting-place, beside his passionate Gordon mother, under the grim, old tower of Hucknall-Torkard. So long indeed do we dwell upon this Byronic episode, as to make of it the virtual *pièce de résistance* in the literary *menu* of these pages.

After the brusque and noisy King William there trails royally into view that Sovereign Victoria, over whose blanched head — in these very June days in which I write — the bells are all ringing a joyous Jubilee for her sixtieth year of reign. But to our eye, and to these pages, she comes as a girl in her teens — modest, yet resolute and calm ; and among her advisers we see the suave and courtly Melbourne ; and among those who make parliamentary battle, in the Queen's young years, that famed historian who has pictured the lives of her kinsfolk — William and Mary — in a way which will make them familiar in the ages to come.

We have a glimpse, too, of the jolly Captain Marryat cracking his for'castle jokes, and of the somewhat tedious, though kindly, G. P. R. James, lifting his chivalric notes about men-at-arms and knightly adventures — a belated hunter in the fields of ancient feudal gramarye.

And with this pennant of the old times of tourney flung to the sharp winds of these days, and shivering in the rude blasts — where anarchic threats lurk and murmur — we close our preface, and bid our readers all welcome to the spread of — what our old friend Dugald Dalgetty would call — the *Vivers.*

D. G. M.

EDGEWOOD, June 24, 1897.

CONTENTS.

CHAPTER I.

CHAPTER II.

CHAPTER III.

CHAPTER IV.

CHAPTER V.

CHAPTER VI.

CHAPTER VII.

ENGLISH LANDS, LETTERS, & KINGS.

CHAPTER I.

THE reader will, perhaps, remember that we brought our last year's ramble amongst British Lands and Letters to an end — in the charming Lake District of England. There, we found Coleridge, before he was yet besotted by his opium-hunger; there, too, we had Church-interview with the stately, silver-haired poet of Rydal Mount — making ready for his last Excursion into the deepest of Nature's mysteries.

The reader will recall, further, how this poet and seer, signalized some of the later years of his life by indignant protests against the schemes —

IV.—1

which were then afoot — for pushing railways among the rural serenities of Westmoreland.

The Lake Country.

It is no wonder; for those Lake counties are very beautiful, — as if, some day, all the tamer features of English landscape had been sifted out, and the residue of picturesqueness and salient objects of flood and mountain had been bunched together in those twin regions of the Derwent and of Windermere. Every American traveller is familiar, of course, with the charming glimpses of Lake Saltonstall from the Shore-line high-road between New York and Boston; let them imagine these multiplied by a score, at frequently recurring intervals of walk or drive; not bald duplications; for sometimes the waters have longer stretch, and the hills have higher reach, and fields have richer culture and more abounding verdure; moreover, occasional gray church towers lift above the trees, and specks of villages whiten spots in the valleys; and the smoothest and hardest of roads run along the margin of the

lakes ; and masses of ivy cover walls, and go riot-
ing all over the fronts of wayside inns. Then,
mountains as high as Graylock, in Berkshire, pile
suddenly out of the quieter undulations of surface, with high-lying ponds in their gulches ;
there are deep swales of heather, and bald rocks,
and gray stone cairns that mark the site of ancient Cumbrian battles.

No wonder that a man loving nature and loving solitude, as Wordsworth did love them, should
have demurred to the project of railways, and
have shuddered — as does Ruskin now — at the
whistling of the demon of civilization among those
hills. But it has come there, notwithstanding,
and come to stay ; and from the station beyond
Bowness, upon the charmingest bit of Windermere, there lies now only an early morning's walk
to the old home of Wordsworth at Rydal. Imme-
diately thereabout, it is true, the levels are a little more puzzling to the engineers, so that the
thirteen miles of charming country road which
stretch thence — twirling hither and yon, and up
and down — in a northwesterly direction to the
town of Keswick and the Derwent valley, remain

now in very much the same condition as when I walked over them, in leisurely way, fifty odd years ago this coming spring. The road in passing out from Rydal village goes near the cottage where poor Hartley Coleridge lived, and earlier, that strange creature De Quincey (of whom we shall have presently more to say) ; it skirts the very margin of Grasmere Lake ; this latter being at your left, while upon the right you can almost see among the near hills the famous "Wishing Gate ;" farther on is Grasmere village, and Grasmere church-yard — in a corner of which is the grave of the old poet, and a modest stone at its head on which is graven only the name, William Words-worth, — as if anything more were needed ! A mile or two beyond, one passes the "Swan Inn," and would like to lodge there, and maybe clamber up Helvellyn, which here shows its great hulk on the right — no miniature mountain, but one which would hold its own (3,000 feet) among the lesser ones which shoulder up the horizon at "Crawford's," in the White Mountains.

Twirling and winding along the flank of Helvellyn, the road comes presently upon the long

Dunmail Rise, where a Cumbrian battle was fought, and where, some six hundred feet above the level of Rydal water, one plunges into mountain savagery. All the while Helvellyn is rising like a giant on the right, and on the left is the lake of Thirlmere, with its shores of precipice. An hour more of easy walking brings one to another crest of hill from which the slope is northward and westward, and from this point you catch sight of the great mass of Skiddaw; while a little hitherward is the white speckle of Keswick town; and stretching away from it to your left lies all the valley of Derwent Water — with a cleft in the hills at its head, down which the brooklet of Lodore comes — "splashing and flashing."

Robert Southey.

I have taken the reader upon this stroll through a bit of the Lake country of England that we might find the poet Dr. Southey * in his old

---

* Robert Southey, b. 1774 ; d. 1843. *Joan of Arc* (pub.) 1796 ; *Thalaba,* 1801; *A Vision of Judgment,* 1821; *Life of Nelson,* 1813 ; *The Doctor,* 1834-47. *Life and Correspondence,* edited by Rev. Chas. Cuthbert Southey, 1849-50.

home at Keswick. It is not properly in the town, but just across the Greta River, which runs southward of the town. There, the modest but goodsized house has been standing for these many years upon a grassy knoll, in its little patch of quiet lawn, with scattered show of trees — but never so many as to forbid full view up the long stretch of Derwent Water. His own hexameters shall tell us something of this view :

"I stood at the window beholding
Mountain and lake and vale ; the valley disrobed of its verdure ;
Derwent, retaining yet from eve a glassy reflection
Where his expanded breast, then still and smooth as a mirror,
Under the woods reposed ; the hills that calm and majestic
Lifted their heads into the silent sky, from far Glaramara,
Bleacrag, and Maidenmawr to Grisedal and westernmost
    Wython,
Dark and distinct they rose. The clouds had gathered above
    them
High in the middle air, huge purple pillowy masses,
While in the West beyond was the last pale tint of the twi-
    light,
Green as the stream in the glen, whose pure and chrysolite
    waters
Flow o'er a schistous bed."

This may be very true picturing ; but it has not the abounding flow of an absorbing rural enthusiasm ; there is too sharp a search in it for the assonance, the spondees and the alliteration—to say nothing of the mineralogy. Indeed, though Southey loved those country ways and heights, of which I have given you a glimpse, and loved his daily walks round about Keswick and the Derwent, and loved the bracing air of the mountains—I think he loved these things as the feeders and comforters of his physical rather than of his spiritual nature. We rarely happen, in his verse, upon such transcripts of out-of-door scenes as are inthralling, and captivate our finer senses; nor does he make the boughs and blossoms tell such stories as filtered through the wood-craft of Chaucer.

Notwithstanding this, it is to that home of Southey, in the beautiful Lake country, that we must go for our most satisfying knowledge of the man. He was so wedded to it; he so loved the murmur of the Greta; so loved his walks; so loved the country freedom; so loved his workaday clothes and cap and his old shoes;* so loved his books —

---

* In a letter to his friend Bedford (he being then aged fifty) he writes: "I have taken again to my old coat and old shoes; dine at the reasonable hour of four; enjoy, as I used to do, the wholesome indulgence of a nap after dinner," etc.

double-deep in his library, and running over into hall and parlor and corridors ; loved, too, the children's voices that were around him there — not his own only, but those always next, and almost his own — those of the young Coleridges.   These were stranded there, with their mother (sister of Mrs. Southey), owing to the rueful neglect of their father — the bard and metaphysician.   I do not think this neglect was due wholly to indifference. Coleridge sidled away from his wife and left her at Keswick in that old home of his own, — where he knew care was good—afraid to encounter her clear, honest, discerning — though unsympathetic — eyes, while he was putting all resources and all subterfuges to the feeding of that opiate craze which had fastened its wolfish fangs upon his very soul.

And Southey had most tender and beautiful care for those half-discarded children of the " Ancient Mariner."   He writes in this playful vein to young Hartley (then aged eleven), who is away on a short visit :

" Mr. Jackson has bought a cow, but he has had no calf since you left him.   Edith [his own daughter] grows like a young giantess, and has a disposition to bite her arm, which you know is a very foolish trick. Your [puppy] friend Dapper, who is, I believe, your God-dog, is in good health, though he grows every summer graver than the last. I am desired to send you as much love as can be enclosed in a letter. I hope it will not be charged double on that account at the post-office. But there is Mrs. Wilson's love, Mr. Jackson's, your Aunt Southey's, your Aunt Lovell's and Edith's; with a *purr* from Bona Marietta [the cat], an open-mouthed kiss from Herbert [the baby], and three wags of the tail from Dapper. I trust they will all arrive safe. Yr. dutiful uncle."

And the same playful humor, and disposition to evoke open-eyed wonderment, runs up and down the lines of that old story of Bishop Hatto and the rats ; and that other smart slap at the barbarities of war — which young people know, or ought to know, as the " Battle of Blenheim " — wherein old Kaspar says,—

> " it was a shocking sight
> After the field was won;
> For many thousand bodies here
> Lay rotting in the sun.
> But things like that, you know, must be,
> After a famous Victory.

> Great praise the Duke of Marlboro' won
> And our good Prince Eugene;

'Why, 'twas a very wicked thing!'
Said little Wilhelmine.
'Nay — nay — my little girl,' quoth he,
'It was a famous Victory.'"

Almost everybody has encountered these South-eyan verses, and that other, about Mary the "Maid of the Inn," in some one or other of the many "collections" of drifting poetry. There are very few, too, who have not, some day, read that most engaging little biography of Admiral Nelson, which tells, in most straightforward and simple and natural way, the romantic story of a life full of heroism, and scored with stains. I do not know, but — with most people — a surer and more lasting memory of Southey would be cherished by reason of those unpretending writings already named, and by knowledge of his quiet, orderly, idyllic home-life among the Lakes of Cumberland — tenderly and wisely provident of the mixed household committed to his care — than by the more ambitious things he did, or by the louder life he lived in the controversialism and politics of the day.

His Early Life.

To judge him more nearly we must give a slight trace of his history. Born down in Bristol (in whose neighborhood we found, you will remember, Chatterton, Mistress More, Coleridge, and others) — he was the son of a broken down linendraper, who could help him little; but a great aunt — a starched woman of the Betsey Trotwood stamp — could and did befriend him, until it came to her knowledge, on a sudden, that he was plotting emigration to the Susquehanna, and plotting marriage with a dowerless girl of Bristol; then she dropped him, and the guardian aunt appears nevermore.

An uncle, however, who is a chaplain in the British service, helps him to Oxford — would have had him take orders — in which case we should have had, of a certainty, some day, Bishop Southey; and probably a very good one. But he has some scruples about the Creed, being overweighted, perhaps, by intercourse with young Coleridge on the side of Unitarianism: " Every atom of grass," he says, "is worth all the Fathers." * He, however, accompanies the uncle to Portugal; dreams dreams and has poetic visions there in the orange-groves of Cintra; projects, too, a History of Portugal — which project unfortunately never comes to fulfilment. He falls in with the United States Minister, General Humphreys, who brings to his notice Dwight's "Conquest of Canaan," which Southey is good enough to think "has some merit."

Thereafter he comes back to his young wife; is much in London and thereabout; coming to know Charles Lamb, Rogers, and Moore, with other such. He is described at that day as tall — a most presentable man — with dark hair and eyes, wonderful arched brows; "head of a poet," Byron said; looking up and off, with proud foretaste of the victories he will win; he has, too, very early, made bold literary thrust at that old story of Joan of Arc : a good topic, of large human interest, but not over successfully dealt with by him. After this came that extraordinary poem of

---

* Letter to Bedford, under date of December, 1793.— *Life and Correspondence*, p. 69.

Thalaba, the first of a triad of poems which excited great literary wonderment (the others being
the *Curse of Kehama* and *Madoc*). They are
rarely heard of now and scarcely known. Beyond
that fragment from *Kehama*, beginning

"They sin who tell us Love can die,"

hardly a page from either has drifted from the
high sea of letters into those sheltered bays where
the makers of anthologies ply their trade. Yet no
weak man could have written either one of these
almost forgotten poems of Southey; recondite
learning makes its pulse felt in them; bright
fancies blaze almost blindingly here and there;
old myths of Arabia and Welsh fables are galvan-
ized and brought to life, and set off with special
knowledge and cumbrous aids of stilted and redundant prosody; but all is utterly remote from
human sympathies, and all as cold — however it
may attract by its glitter — as the dead hand

" Shrivelled, and dry, and black,"

which holds the magic taper in the Dom Daniel
cavern of *Thalaba*.

A fourth long poem — written much later in life — *Roderick the Goth*, has a more substantial basis of human story, and so makes larger appeal to popular interest; but it had never a marked success.

Meantime, Southey has not kept closely by London; there have been peregrinations, and huntings for a home — for children and books must have a settlement. Through friends of influence he had come to a fairly good political appointment in Ireland, but has no love for the bulls and blunderbusses which adorn life there; nor will he tutor his patron's boys — which also comes into the scale of his duties — so gives up that chance of a livelihood. There is, too, a new trip to Portugal with his wife; and a new reverent and dreamy listening to the rustle of the shining leaves of the orange-trees of Cintra. I do not think those murmurous tales of the trees of Portugal, burdened with old monastic flavors, ever went out of his ears wholly till he died. But finally the poet does come to settlement, somewhere about 1803 — in that Keswick home, where we found him at the opening of our chapter.

˙*Greta Hall.*

Coleridge is for awhile a fellow-tenant with him there, then blunders away to Grasmere — to London, to Highgate, and into that over-strained, disorderly life of which we know so much and yet not enough. But Southey does not lack self-possession, or lack poise : he has not indeed so much brain to keep on balance ; but he thinks excellently well of his own parts ; he is disgusted when people look up to him after his Irish appointment — "as if," he said, "the author of *Joan of Arc,* and of *Thalaba,* were made a great man by scribing for the Chancellor of the Exchequer."

Yet for that poem of *Thalaba,* in a twelve-month after issue, he had only received as his share of profits a matter of £3 15s. Indeed, Southey would have fared hardly money-wise in those times, if he had not won the favor of a great many good and highly placed friends ; and it was only four years after his establishment at Keswick, when these friends succeeded in securing to him

an annual Government pension of £200. Landor
had possibly aided him before this time ; he certainly had admired greatly his poems and given
praise that would have been worth more, if he had
not spoiled it by rating Southey as a poet so much
above Byron, Scott, and Coleridge.*

In addition to these aids the *Quarterly Review*
was set afoot in those days in London — of which
sturdy defender of Church and State, Southey
soon became a virtual pensioner. Moreover, with
his tastes, small moneys went a long way ; he was
methodical to the last degree ; he loved his old
coats and habits ; he loved his marches and count-

---

* In the *Imaginary Conversation* between Southey and
Porson, Landor makes Porson say : " It is pleasant to find
two poets [Southey and Wordsworth] living as brothers, and
particularly when the palm lies between them, with hardly a
third in sight."

Lamb, too, in a letter to Mr. Coleridge (p. 194, Moxon edition of 1832, London), says : " On the whole, I expect Southey
one day to rival Milton ; I already deem him equal to Cowper,
and superior to all living poets besides." This is *apropos* of
Joan of Arc, which had then recently appeared. He begins
his letter : " With *Joan of Arc* I have been delighted,
amazed ; I had not presumed to expect anything of such ex-
cellence from Southey."

ermarches among the hills that flank Skiddaw
better than he loved horses, or dogs, or guns; a
quiet evening in his library with his books, was
always more relished than ever so good a place at
Drury Lane. New friends and old brighten that
retirement for him. He has his vacation runs to
Edinboro'—to London—to Bristol; the children
are growing (though there is death of one little
one—away from home); the books are piling up
in his halls in bigger and always broader ranks.
He writes of Brazil, of Spanish matters, of new
poetry, of Nelson, of Society—showing touches
of his early radicalism, and of a Utopian humor,
which age and the heavy harness of conventional-
ism he has learned to wear, do not wholly destroy.
He writes of Wesley and of the Church—settled
in those maturer years into a comfortable routine-
ordered Churchism, which does not let too airy a
conscience prick him into unrest. A good, safe
monarchist, too, who comes presently, and rightly
enough—through a suggestion of George IV.,
then Regent in place of crazy George III.*—by

---

* George IV. was appointed Regent in the year 1811, the
old king, George III., being then plainly so far bereft of his

his position as Poet Laureate; and in that capacity writes a few dismally stiff odes, which are his worst work.   Even Wordsworth, who walks over those Cumberland hills with reverence, and with a pious fondness traces the " star-shaped shadows on the naked stones" — cannot warm to Southey's new gush over royalty in his New Year's Odes. Coleridge chafes; and Landor, we may be sure, sniffs, and swears, with a great roar of voice, at what looks so like to sycophancy.

To this time belongs that ode whose vengeful lines, after the fall of Napoleon, whip round the Emperor's misdeeds in a fury of Tory Anglicanism, and call on France to avenge her wrongs :— !

> " By the lives which he hath shed,
>   By the ruin he hath spread,
>   By the prayers which rise for curses on his head—

---

senses as to incapacitate him even for intelligent clerical service.   He died, as we shall find later, in the year 1820, when the Regent succeeded, and reigned for ten years.

The *Croker Papers* (1884), recently published, make mention of Mr. Croker's intervention in the matter of the bestowal of the Laureate-ship upon Southey.   Croker was an old friend of Southey, and a trusted go-between in all literary service for the royal household.

Redeem, O France, thine ancient fame!
Revenge thy sufferings and thy shame!
Open thine eyes! Too long hast thou been blind!
Take vengeance for thyself and for mankind!"

This seems to me only the outcry of a tempestuous British scold ; and yet a late eulogist has the effrontery to name it in connection with the great prayerful burst of Milton upon the massacre of the Waldenses :—

" Avenge, O Lord, thy slaughtered saints whose bones
Lie scattered on the Alpine mountains cold."

No, no ; Southey was no Milton—does not reach to the height of an echo of Milton.

Yet he was a rare and accomplished man of books — of books rather than genius, I think. An excellent type of the very clever and well-trained professional writer, working honestly and steadily in the service to which he has put himself. Very politic, too, in his personal relations. Even Carlyle — for a wonder — speaks of him without lacerating him.

In a certain sense he was not insincere ; yet he had none of that outspoken exuberant sincerity which breaks forth in declaratory speech, before the public time-pieces have told us how to pitch

our voices.   Landor had this : so had Coleridge.
Southey never would have run away from his wife
— never; he might dislike her; but Society's great
harness (if nothing more) would hold him in
check ; there were conditions under which Coleridge might and did.   Southey would never over-
drink or over-tipple; there were conditions (not
rare) under which Coleridge might and did.   Yet,
for all this, I can imagine a something finer in
the poet of the *Ancient Mariner* — that felt moral
chafings far more cruelly; and for real poetic
unction you might put *Thalaba,* and *Kehama,*
and *Madoc* all in one scale, and only *Christabel*
in the other — and the Southey poems would be
bounced out of sight.   But how many poets of
the century can put a touch to verse like the
touch in *Christabel?*

The Doctor and Last Shadows.

I cannot forbear allusion to that curious book —
little read now — which was published by Southey
anonymously, called *The Doctor :* * a book show-

* The sixth and seventh volumes appeared after the poet's
death, in 1817.

ing vast accumulation of out-of-the-way bits of learning — full of quips, and conceits, and oddities; there are traces of Sterne in it and of Rabelais; but there is little trenchant humor of its own. It is a literary jungle; and all its wit sparkles like marsh fire-flies that lead no whither. You may wonder at its erudition; wonder at its spurts of meditative wisdom; wonder at its touches of scholastic cleverness, and its want of any effective coherence, but you wonder more at its waste of power. Yet he had great pride in this book; believed it would be read admiringly long after him; enjoyed vastly a boyish dalliance — if not a lying by-play — with the secret of its authorship; but he was, I think, greatly aggrieved by its want of the brilliant success he had hoped for.

But sorrows of a more grievous sort were dawning on him. On the very year before the publication of the first volumes of *The Doctor,* he writes to his old friend, Bedford: "I have been parted from my wife by something worse than death. Forty years she has been the life of my life; and I have left her this day in a lunatic asylum."

But she comes back within a year — quiet, but all beclouded ; looking vacantly upon the faces of the household, saddened, and much thinned now. For the oldest boy Herbert is dead years since ; and the daughter, Isabel, "the most radiant creature (he says) that I ever beheld, or shall behold" — dead too ; his favorite niece, Sara Coleridge, married and gone ; his daughter Edith, married and gone ; and now that other Edith — his wife — looking with an idle stare around the almost empty house. It was at this juncture, when all but courage seemed taken from him, that Sir Robert Peel wrote, offering the poet a Baronetcy ; but he was beyond taking heart from any such toy as this. He must have felt a grim complacency — now that his hair was white and his shoulders bowed by weight of years and toil, and his home so nearly desolate — in refusing the empty bauble which Royalty offered, and in staying — plain Robert Southey.

Presently thereafter his wife died ; and he, whose life had been such a domestic one, strayed round the house purposeless, like a wheel spinning blindly — off from its axle. Friends, however, took him away with them to Paris; among these friends — that always buoyant and companionable Crabb Robinson, whose diary is so rich in reminiscences of the literary men of these times. Southey's son Cuthbert went with him, and the poet made a good mock of enjoying the new scenes; plotted great work again — did labor heartily on his return, and two years thereafter committed the indiscretion of marrying again: the loneliness at Keswick was so great. The new mistress he had long known and esteemed; and she (Miss Caroline Bowles) was an excellent, kindly, judicious woman — although a poetess.

But it was never a festive house again. All the high lights in that home picture which was set between Skiddaw and the Derwent-water were blurred. Wordsworth, striding across the hills by Dunmail Rise, on one of his rare visits, reports that Southey is all distraught; can talk of nothing but his books; and presently — counting only by months — it appears that he will not even talk of these — will talk of nothing. His hand-writing, which had been neat — of which he had been proud — went all awry in a great scrawl obliquely athwart the page. For a year or two he is in this lost trail; mumbling, but not talking; seeing things — yet as one who sees not; clinging to those loved books of his — fondling them; passing up and down the library to find this or the other volume that had been carefully cherished — taking them from their shelves; putting his lips to them — then replacing them; — a year or more of this automatic life — the light in him all quenched.

He died in 1843, and was buried in the pretty church-yard of Crosthwaite, a short mile away from his old home. Within the church is a beautiful recumbent figure of the poet, which every traveller should see.

Crabb Robinson.

I had occasion to name Crabb Robinson * as one of the party accompanying Southey on his last visit to the Continent. Robinson was a man whom it is well to know something of, by reason

---

* Henry Crabb Robinson, b. 1775; d. 1867. *Diary, Reminiscences*, etc. (ed. by Sadler), 1869.

of his Boswell-ian *Reminiscences*, and because —
though of comparatively humble origin — he grew
to be an excellent type of the well-bred, well-read
club-man of his day — knowing everybody who
was worth knowing, from Mrs. Siddons to Walter
Scott, and talking about everybody who was worth
talking of, from Louis Phillippe to Mrs. Barbauld.

He was quick, of keen perception — always
making the most of his opportunities; had fair
schooling; gets launched somehow upon an attor-
ney's career, to which he never took with great
enthusiasm. He was an apt French scholar —
passed four or five years, too, studying in Ger-
many; his assurance and intelligence, aptitude,
and good-nature bringing him to know almost
everybody of consequence. He is familiar with
Madame de Staël — hob-nobs with many of the
great German writers of the early part of this century — is for a time correspondent of the *Times*
from the Baltic and Stockholm; and from Spain
also, in the days when Bonaparte is raging over
the Continent. He returns to London, revives
old acquaintances, and makes new ones; knows
Landor and Dyer and Campbell; is hail fellow

—as would seem —with Wordsworth, Southey, Moore, and Lady Blessington ; falls into some helpful legacies ; keeps lazily by his legal practice ; husbands his resources, but never marries ; pounces upon every new lion of the day ; hears Coleridge lecture ; hears Hazlitt lecture ; hears Erskine plead, and goes to play whist and drink punch with the Lambs. He was full of anecdote, and could talk by the hour. Rogers once said to his guests who were prompt at breakfast : "If you've anything to say, you'd better say it ; Crabb Robinson is coming." He talked on all subjects with average acuteness, and more than average command of language, and little graceful subtleties of social speech — but with no special or penetrative analysis of his subject-matter. The very type of a current, popular, well-received man of the town — good at cards — good at a club dinner — good at supper — good in travel — good for a picnic — good for a lady's tea-fight.

He must have written reams on reams of letters. The big books of his *Diary and Reminiscences* *

---

* Best edition is that of Macmillan, London, 1869.

which I commend to you for their amusing and most entertaining gossip, contained only a most inconsiderable part of his written leavings.

He took admirable care of himself; did not permit exposure to draughts — to indigestions, or to bad company of any sort. Withal he was charitable — was particular and fastidious; always knew the best rulings of society about ceremony, and always obeyed; never wore a dress-coat counter to good form. He was an excellent listener — especially to people of title; was a judicious flatterer — a good friend and a good fellow; dining out five days in the week, and living thus till ninety: and if he had lived till now, I think he would have died — dining out.

Mr. Robinson was not very strong in literary criticism. I quote a bit from his *Diary*, that will show, perhaps as well as any, his method and range. It is dated *June 6, 1812* :

"Sent *Peter Bell* to Chas. Lamb. To my surprise, he does not like it. He complains of the slowness of the narrative — as if that were not the *art* of the poet. He says Wordsworth has great thoughts, but has left them out here. [And then continues in his own person.] In the perplexity arising from the diverse judgments of those to whom I am accustomed to look up, I have no resource but in the determination to disregard all opinions, and trust to the simple impression made on my own mind. When Lady Mackintosh was once stating to Coleridge her disregard of the beauties of nature, which men commonly affect to admire, he said his friend Wordsworth had described her feeling, and quoted three lines from ' *Peter Bell:* '

> ' A primrose by a river brim
> ' A yellow primrose was to him,
> ' And it was nothing more.'

"'Yes,' said Lady Mackintosh — 'that is precisely my case.' "

Thomas De Quincey.

On the same page of that *Diary* — where I go to verify this quotation — is this entry :

"At four o'clock dined in the [Temple] Hall with De Quincey, * who was very civil to me, and cordially invited me to visit his cottage in Cumberland. Like myself, he is an enthusiast for Wordsworth. His person is small, his complexion fair, and his air and manner are those of a sickly and enfeebled man." †

---

* Thomas De Quincey, b. 1785; d. 1859. *Confessions of an English Opium Eater*, 1821. Complete edition of works, 1852-55. *Life and Writings:* H. A. Page, 2 vols. London, 1877.

† The entry is of 1812, p. 391, chap. **xv.** Macmillan's edition. London, 1869.

Some twenty-seven years before the date of this encounter, the sickly looking man was born near to Manchester, his father being a well-to-do merchant there — whose affairs took him often to Portugal and Madeira, and whose invalidism kept him there so much that the son scarce knew him ; — remembers only how his father came home one day to his great country house — pale, and propped up with pillows in the back of his carriage — came to die. His mother, left with wealth enough for herself and children, was of a stern Calvinistic sort ; which fact gives a streak of unpleasant color here and there to the son's reminiscences. He is presently at odds with her about the Bath school — where he is taught — she having moved into Somersetshire, whereabout she knows Mistress Hannah More ; the boy comes to know this lady too, with much reverence. The son is at odds with his mother again about Eton (where, though never a scholar, he has glimpses of George III. — gets a little grunted talk even, from the old king) — and is again at odds with the mother about the Manchester Grammar School : so much at odds here, that he takes the bit fairly in his mouth, and runs away with *Eurip-ides* in his pocket. Then he goes wandering in Wales — gypsy-like — and from there strikes across country blindly to London, where he becomes gypsy indeed. He bargains with Jews to advance money on his expectations : and with this money for "sinker," he sounds a depth of sin and misery which we may guess at, by what we know, but which in their fulness, even his galloping pen never told. Into some of those depths his friends traced him, and patched up a truce, which landed him in Oxford.

Quiet and studious here at first — he is represented as a rare talker, a little given to wine — writing admiring letters to Wordsworth and others, who were his gods in those days ; falling somehow into taste for that drug which for so many years held him in its grip, body and soul. The Oxford career being finished after a sort, there are saunterings through London streets again — evenings with the Lambs, with Godwin, and excursions to Somersetshire and the Lake country, where he encounters and gives nearer worship to the poetic gods of his idolatry. Al-

ways shy, but earnest ; most interesting to strangers — with his pale face, high brow and lightning
glances ; talking too with a winning flow and an
exuberance of epithet that somewhiles amounts to
brilliancy : no wonder he was tenderly entreated
by good Miss Wordsworth ; no wonder the poet
of the "Doe of Rylstone" enjoyed the titillation
of such fresh, bright praises !

So De Quincey at twenty-four became house-
holder near to Grasmere — in the cottage I spoke
of in the opening of the chapter — once occupied
by Wordsworth, and later by Hartley Coleridge.
There, on that pretty shelf of the hills — scarce
lifted above Rydal-water, he gathers his books —
studies the mountains — provokes the gossip of
all the pretty Dalesmen's daughters — lives there
a bachelor, eight years or more — ranging round
and round in bright autumnal days with the
sturdy John Wilson (of the *Noctes Ambrosianæ*)
— cultivating intimacy with poor crazy Lloyd
(who lived nearby) — studying all anomalous characters with curious intensity, and finding anom-
alies where others found none. Meantime and
through all, his sensibilities are kept wrought

to fever heat by the opiate drinks — always flank-
ing him at his table ; and he, so dreadfully wonted
to those devilish drafts, that — on some occasions
— he actually consumes within the twenty-four
hours the equivalent of seven full wine-glasses
of laudanum ! No wonder the quiet Dales-people
looked dubiously at the light burning in those
cottage windows far into the gray of morning,
and counted the pale-faced, big-headed man for
something uncanny.

In these days comes about that strange episode
of his mad attachment to the little elfin child —
Catharine Wordsworth — of whom the poet-father
wrote :—

> "Solitude to her
> Was blithe society, who filled the air
> With gladness and involuntary songs.
> Light were her sallies, as the tripping fawn's,
> Forth startled from the form where she lay couched ;
> Unthought of, unexpected, as the stir
> Of the soft breeze ruffling the meadow flowers."

Yet De Quincey, arrogantly interpreting the
deep-seated affections of that father's heart, says,
" She was no favorite with Wordsworth ;" but he
" himself was blindly, doatingly, fascinated " by

this child of three. And of her death, before she is four, when De Quincey is on a visit in London, he says, with crazy exaggeration :

"Never, perhaps, from the foundations of those mighty hills was there so fierce a convulsion of grief as mastered my faculties on receiving that heart-shattering news. . . . I had always viewed her as an impersonation of the dawn and the spirit of infancy. . . . I returned hastily to Grasmere; stretched myself every night, for more than two months running, upon her grave; in fact often passed the night upon her grave . . . in mere intensity of sick, frantic yearning after neighborhood to the darling of my heart." *

This is a type of his ways of feeling, and of his living, and of his speech—tending easily to all manner of extravagance : black and white are too tame for his nerve-exaltation ; if a friend looks sharply, "his eye glares;" if disturbed, he has a "tumult of the brain;" if he doubles his fist, his gestures are the wildest ; and a well-built son and daughter of a neighbor Dalesman are the images of "Coriolanus and Valeria."

---

* Page 215; vol. ii., *Reminiscences.* Boston Edition.

Marriage and other Flights.

At thirty-one, or thereabout, De Quincey married the honest daughter of an honest yeoman of the neighborhood. She was sensible (except her marriage invalidate the term), was kindly, was long-suffering, and yet was very human. I suspect the interior of that cottage was not always like the islands of the blessed. Mr. Froude would perhaps have enjoyed lifting the roof from such a house. Many children were born to that strangely coupled pair,—some of them still living and most worthy.

It happens by and by to this impractical man, from whose disorderly and always open hand inherited moneys have slipped away; it happens — I say — that he must earn his bread by his own toil; so he projects great works of philosophy, of political economy, which are to revolutionize opinions; but they topple over into opium dreams before they are realized. He tries editing a county paper, but it is nought. At last he utilizes even his vices, and a chapter of the *Confessions of an Opium Eater*, in the *London Magazine*, draws swift attention to one whose language is as vivid as a flame ; and he lays bare, without qualm, his own quivering sensibilities. This spurt of work, or some new craze, takes him to London, away from his family. And so on a sudden, that idyl of life among the Lakes becomes for many years a tattered and blurred page to him. He is once more a denizen of the great city, living a shy, hermit existence there ; long time in a dim backroom of the publisher Bohn's, in Bedford Street, near to Covent Garden. He sees Proctor and Hazlitt odd-whiles, and Hood, and still more of the Lambs ; but he is peevish and distant, and finds largest company in the jug of laudanum which brings swift succeeding dreams and stupefaction.

We will have a taste of some of his wild writing of those days. He is speaking of a dream.

" The dream commenced with a music of preparation and of awakening suspense ; a music like the opening of the Coronation Anthem, and which, like that, gave the feeling of a vast march ; of infinite cavalcades filing off, and the tread of innumerable armies. The morning was come of a mighty day, a day of crisis and of final hope for human nature, then suffering some mysterious eclipse, and laboring in some

dread extremity. Somewhere, I knew not where—somehow, I
knew not how—by some beings, I knew not whom—a battle,
a strife, an agony was conducting, was evolving like a great
drama or a piece of music. . . . I had the power, and
yet had not the power to decide it . . . for the weight of
twenty Atlantes was upon me as the oppression of inexpiable
guilt. Deeper than ever plummet sounded, I lay inactive.
Then, like a chorus, the passion deepened; there came sudden
alarms, hurrying to and fro, trepidations of innumerable
fugitives, I know not whether from the good cause or the
bad; darkness and lights; tempest and human faces; and at
last, with the sense that all was lost, female forms, and the
features that were worth all the world to me, and but a moment allowed — and clasped hands and heart-breaking part-
ings, and then everlasting farewells! and with a sigh such as
the caves of hell sighed when the incestuous mother uttered
the abhorred name of Death, the sound was reverberated —
everlasting farewells! and again, and yet again reverberated
— everlasting farewells!"

Some years later he drifts again to Grasmere,
but only to pluck up root and branch that home
with wife and children,—so wonted now to the
pleasant sounds and sights of the Lake waters and
the mountains—and to transport them to Edinboro', where, through Professor Wilson, he has
promise of work which had begun to fail him in
London.

There,—though he has the introduction which

a place at the tavern table of Father Ambrose gives—he is a lonely man; pacing solitary, sometimes in the shadow of the Castle Rock, sometimes in the shadow of the old houses of the Canongate; always preoccupied, close-lipped, brooding, and never without that wretched opium-comforter at his home. It was in *Blackwood* (1827) he first published the well known essay on "Murder as a Fine Art,"—perhaps the best known of all he wrote; there, too, he committed to paper, in the stress of his necessities, those sketchy *Reminiscences* of his Lake life; loose, disjointed, ill-considered, often sent to press without any revision and full of strange coined words. I note at random, such as *novel-ish erector* (for builder), *lambencies, apricating, aculeated;* using words not rarely, etymologically, and for some recondite sense attaching. Worse than this, there is dreary tittle-tattle and a pulling away of decent domestic drapery from the lives of those he had professed to love and honor; tedious expatiation, too, upon the scandal-mongering of servant-maids, with illustrations by page on page; and yet, for the matter of gossip, he is himself as fertile as a seamstress or a

monthly nurse, and as overflowing and brazen as
any newspaper you may name.

But here and there, even amid his dreariest
pages, you see, quivering — some gleams of his
old strange power — a thrust of keen thought
that bewilders you by its penetration — a glowing
fancy that translates one to wondrous heights of
poetic vision ; and oftener yet, and over and over,
shows that mastery of the finesse of language by
which he commands the most attenuated reaches
of his thought, and whips them into place with
a snap and a sting.

Yet, when all is said, I think we must count
the best that he wrote only amongst the curiosities of literature, rather than with the manna
that fell for fainting souls in the wilderness.

De Quincey died in Edinburgh, in 1859, aged
seventy-four.

CHAPTER II.

IN our last chapter we took a breezy morning walk amid the Lake scenery of England — more particularly that portion of it which lies between the old homes of Wordsworth and of Southey; we found it a thirteen-mile stretch of road, coiling along narrow meadows and over gray heights — beside mountains and mountain tarns — with Helvellyn lifting mid-way and Skiddaw towering at the end. We had our talk of Dr. Southey — so brave at his work — so generous in his home charities — so stiff in his Churchism and latter-day Toryism — with a very keen eye for beauty; yet writing poems — stately and masterful — which long ago went to the top-shelves, and stay there.

We had our rough and ready interviews with that first of "War Correspondents" — Henry

Crabb Robinson — who knew all the prominent
men of this epoch, and has given us such entertaining chit-chat about them, as we all listen
to, and straightway forget. Afterwards we had
a look at that strange, intellectual, disorderly
creature De Quincey — he living a long while in
the Lake Country — and in his more inspired
moments seeming to carry us by his swift words,
into that mystical region lying beyond the borders
of what we know and see. He swayed men; but
he rarely taught them, or fed them.

Christopher North.

We still linger about those charmingest of
country places; and by a wooden gateway — ad-
joining the approach to Windermere Hotel —
enter upon the " Elleray woods," amid which
lived — eighty years ago — that stalwart friend of
De Quincey's, whose acquaintance he made among
the Lakes, and who, like himself, was a devoted
admirer of Wordsworth. Indeed, I think it was
at the home of the latter that De Quincey first
encountered the tall, lusty John Wilson — brimful of enthusiasm and all country ardors; brimful,

too, of gush, and all poetic undulations of speech.
He * was a native of Paisley — his father having
been a rich manufacturer there — and had come to
spend his abundant enthusiasms and his equally
abundant moneys between Wordsworth and the
mountains and Windermere. He has his fleet
of yachts and barges upon the lake ; he knows
every pool where any trout lurk — every height
that gives far-off views. He is a pugilist, a
swimmer, an oarsman — making the hills echo
with his jollity, and dashing off through the
springy heather with that slight, seemingly frail
De Quincey in his wake—who only reaches to his
shoulder, but who is all compact of nerve and
muscle. For Greek they are fairly mated, both
by love and learning ; and they can and do chant
together the choral songs of heathen tragedies.

This yellow-haired, blue-eyed giant, John Wil-

---

* John Wilson, b. 1785 ; d. 1854 ; better known as Christopher North, his pseudonym in *Blackwood*. *The Isle of
Palms,* 1811 ; *The City of the Plague,* 1816 ; *Recreations of
Christopher North,* 1842. In 1851 a civil-list pension of
£300 was conferred upon him. His younger brother James
Wilson was a well-known naturalist, and author of *The Rod
and the Gun.*

son — not so well-known now as he was sixty years
ago — we collegians greatly admired in that far-off
day.   He had written the *Isle of Palms,* and was
responsible for much of the wit and dash and
merriment which sparkled over the early pages
of *Blackwood's Magazine* — in the chapters of the
Noctes Ambrosianæ and in many a paper besides :
— he had his first university training at Glasgow ;
had a brief love-episode there also, which makes
a prettily coy appearance on the pleasant pages
of the biography of Wilson which a daughter
(Mrs. Gordon) has compiled.   After Glasgow came
Oxford ; and a characteristic bit of his later writing, which I cite, will show you how Oxford impressed him : —

"Having bidden farewell to our sweet native Scotland,
and kissed ere we parted, the grass and the flowers with a
show of filial tears — having bidden farewell to all her glens,
now a-glimmer in the blended light of imagination and
memory, with their cairns and kirks, their low-chimneyed
huts, and their high-turreted halls, their free-flowing rivers,
and lochs dashing like seas — we were all at once buried not
in the Cimmerian gloom, but the Cerulean glitter of Oxford's
Ancient Academic groves.   The genius of the place fell upon
us.   Yes! we hear now, in the renewed delight of the awe of
our youthful spirit, the pealing organ in that Chapel called

the Beautiful; we see the Saints on the stained windows; at
the Altar the picture of One up Calvary meekly ascending.
It seemed then that our hearts had no need even of the kind-
ness of kindred — of the country where we were born, and
that had received the continued blessings of our enlarging
love ! Yet away went, even then, sometimes, our thoughts
to Scotland, like carrier-pigeons wafting love messages beneath their unwearied wings." *

We should count this, and justly, rather over-
fine writing nowadays. Yet it is throughout
stamped with the peculiarities of Christopher
North ; he cannot help his delightfully wanton
play with language and sentiment ; and into whatever sea of topics he plunged — early or late in
life — he always came up glittering with the beads
and sparkles of a highly charged rhetoric. Close
after Oxford comes that idyllic life † in Winder-

---

* "Old North and Young North." *Blackwood*, June, 1828.

† Dorothy Wordsworth, under date of 1809, writes to her
friend, Lady Beaumont — "Surely I have spoken to you of
Mr. Wilson, a young man of some fortune, who has built a
house in a very fine situation not far from Bowness. . . .
He has from boyhood been a passionate admirer of my
brother's writings. [And again.] We all, including Mr.
De Quincey and Coleridge, have been to pay the Bachelor
(Wilson) a visit, and we enjoyed ourselves very much in a

mere to which I have referred. Four or more
years pass there; his trees grow there; his new
roads — hewn through the forests — wind there;
he plots a new house there; he climbs the mountains; he is busy with his boats. Somewhat later
he marries; he does not lose his old love for the
poets of the Greek anthology; he has children
born to him; he breeds game fowls, and looks
after them as closely as a New England farmer's
wife after her poultry; but with him poetry and
poultry go together. There are old diaries of his
— into which his daughter gives us a peep — that
show such entries as this : — " The small Paisley
hen set herself 6th of July, with no fewer than
nine eggs;" and again — " Red pullet in Josie's
barn was set with eight eggs on Thursday;" and
square against such memoranda, and in script as
careful, will appear some bit of verse like this : —

> " Oh, fairy child! what can I wish for thee ?
> Like a perennial flowret may'st thou be,

---

pleasant mixture of merriment, and thoughtful discourse.
. . . He is now twenty-three years of age."—Colcorton *Letters*, vol. ii, p. 91.

That spends its life in beauty and in bliss ;
Soft on thee fall the breath of time,
And still retain in heavenly clime
The bloom that charms in this."

He wrote, too, while living there above Windermere, his poem of the *Isle of Palms;* having a fair success in the early quarter of this century, but which was quickly put out of sight and hearing by the brisker, martial music of Scott, and by the later and more vigorous and resonant verse of Byron.

Indeed, Wilson's poetry was not such as we would have looked for from one who was a "varra bad un to lick" at a wrestling bout, and who made the splinters fly when his bludgeon went thwacking into a page of controversial prose. His verse is tender ; it is graceful ; it is delicate ; it is full of languors too ; and it is tiresome — a gentle girlish treble of sound it has, that you can hardly associate with this brawny mass of manhood.

Wilson in Scotland.

But all that delightful life amidst the woods of Elleray — with its game-cocks, and boats, and

mountain rambles, and shouted chorus of Prometheus — comes to a sharp end. The inherited
fortune of the poet, by some criminal careless-
ness or knavery of a relative, goes in a day; and
our fine stalwart wrestler must go to Edinboro'
to wrestle with the fates. There he coquets
for a time with law; but presently falls into
pleasant affiliation with old Mr. Blackwood (who
was a remarkable man in his way) in the conduct
of his magazine. And then came the trumpet
blasts of mingled wit, bravado, and tenderness,
which broke into those pages, and which made
young college men in England or Scotland or
America, fling up their hats for Christopher
North. Not altogether a safe guide, I think,
as a rhetorician; too much bounce in him; too
little self-restraint; too much of glitter and irides-
cence; but, on the other hand — bating some
blackguardism — he is brimful of life and hearti-
ness and merriment — lighted up with scholarly
hues of color.

There was associated with Wilson in those days,
in work upon *Blackwood*, a young man — whom
we may possibly not have occasion to speak of

again, and yet who is worthy of mention. I mean
J. G. Lockhart,* who afterwards became son-in-
law and the biographer of Walter Scott — a slight
young fellow in that day, very erect and prim ;
wearing his hat well forward on his heavy brows,
and so shading a face that was thin, clean cut,
handsome, and which had almost the darkness
of a Spaniard's. He put his rapier-like thrusts
into a good many papers which the two wrought
at together. All his life he loved literary digs
with his stiletto — which was very sharp — and
when he left Edinboro to edit the *Quarterly
Review* in London (as he did in after days) he
took his stiletto with him. There are scenes in
that unevenly written Lockhart story of *Adam
Blair* — hardly known now — which for thrilling
passion, blazing out of clear sufficiencies of
occasion, would compare well with kindred scenes
of Scott's own, and which score deeper colorings

---

*John Gibson Lockhart, b. 1794 ; d. 1854. Connected
with *Blackwood*, 1818 ; *Adam Blair*, 1822; with *Quarterly
Review*, 1826–53 ; *Ancient Spanish Ballads*, 1823 ; *Memoirs
of Walter Scott*, 1836–38. Recent *Life of Lockhart*, by Andrew Lang. 2 vols., 8vo. Nimmo, London.

of human woe and loves and remorse than belong
to most modern stories ; not lighted, indeed, with
humor ; not entertaining with anecdote ; not embroidered with archæologic knowledge ; not rat-
tling with coruscating social fireworks, but —
subtle, psychologic, touching the very marrow of
our common manhood with a pen both sharp and
fine. We remember him, however, most gratefully
as the charming biographer of Scott, and as the
accomplished translator of certain Spanish ballads
into which he has put — under flowing English
verse — all the clashing of Cordovan castanets,
and all the jingle of the war stirrups of the Moors.

We return now to Professor Wilson and propose
to tell you how he came by that title. It was
after only a few years of work in connection
with *Blackwood* that the Chair of Moral Philosophy in Edinboro' University — which had been
held by Dugald Stewart, and later by Dr. Thomas
Brown — fell vacant ; and at once the name of
Wilson was pressed by his friends for the position.
It was not a little odd that a man best known by
two delicate poems, and by a bold swashbuckler
sort of magazine writing should be put forward

— in such a staid city as Edinboro', and against
such a candidate as Sir William Hamilton — for a
Chair which had been held by Dugald Stewart!
But he *was* so put forward, and successfully;
Walter Scott and the Government coming to his
aid. Upon this, he went resolutely to study in
the new line marked out for him; his rods and
guns were, for the time, hung upon the wall; his
wrestling frolics and bouts at quarter-staff, and
suppers at the Ambrose tavern, were laid under
limitations. He put a conscience and a pertinacity into his labor that he had never put to any
intellectual work before.* But there were very

---

* Mrs. Gordon says, quoting from her mother's record :
Mr. Wilson is as busy studying as possible ; indeed, he has
little time before him for his great task ; he says it will take
one month at least to make out a catalogue of the books he
has to read and consult. I am perfectly appalled when I go
into the dining-room and see all the folios, quartos, and
duodecimos, with which it is literally filled ; and the poor
culprit himself sitting in the midst, with a beard as long and
red as an ancient carrot; for he has not shaved for a fort-
night. P. 215, *Memoir of John Wilson.* We are sorry to see
that Mr. Lang, in his recent *Life of Lockhart* (1897), pp.
135-6-7-8, has put some disturbing cross-coloring (perhaps
justly) upon the pleasant portrait which Mrs. Gordon has
drawn of Christopher North.

IV.—4

many people in Edinboro' who had been aggrieved by the appointment — largely, too, among those from whom his pupils would come. There was, naturally, great anxiety among his friends respecting the opening of the first session. An eye-witness says : —

"I went prepared to join in a cabal which was formed to put him down. The lecture-room was crowded to the ceiling. Such a collection of hard-browed, scowling Scotsmen, muttering over their knob-sticks, I never saw. The Professor entered with a bold step, amid profound silence. Every one expected some deprecatory, or propitiatory introduction of himself and his subject, upon which the mass was to decide against him, reason or no reason; but he began with a voice of thunder right into the matter of his lecture, kept up—unflinchingly and unhesitatingly, without a pause— a flow of rhetoric such as Dugald Stewart or Dr. Brown, his predecessors, never delivered in the same place. Not a word — not a murmur escaped his captivated audience; and at the end they gave him a right-down unanimous burst of applause." *

From that time forth, for thirty years or more, John Wilson held the place, and won a popularity

---

* Mrs. Gordon's *Memoir of John Wilson*, p. 222. The statement is credited to the author of *The Two Cosmos.* Middleton, New York, 1863.

with his annual relays of pupils that was un-exampled and unshaken. Better lectures in his province may very possibly have been written by others elsewhere — more close, more compact, more thoroughly thought out, more methodic. His were not patterned after Reid and Stewart; indeed, not patterned at all; not wrought into a burnished system, with the pivots and cranks of the old school-men all in their places. But they made up a series — continuous, and lapping each into each, by easy confluence of topic — of discourses on moral duties and on moral relations, with full and brilliant illustrative talk — some-times in his heated moments taking on the gush and exuberance of a poem; other times bristling with reminiscences; yet full of suggestiveness, and telling as much, I think, on the minds of his eager and receptive students as if the rhetorical brilliancies had all been plucked away, and some master of a duller craft had reduced his words to a stiff, logical paradigm.

From this time forward Professor Wilson lived a quiet, domestic, yet fully occupied life. He wrote enormously for the magazine with which

his name had become identified ; there is scarce a
break in his thirty years' teachings in the university ; there are sometimes brief interludes of travel ;
journeys to London ; flights to the Highlands ;
there are breaks in his domestic circle, breaks in
the larger circle of his friends ; there are twinges
of the gout and there come wrinkles of age ; but
he is braver to resist than most ; and for years on
years everybody knew that great gaunt figure, with
blue eyes and hair flying wild, striding along Edinboro streets.

His poems have indeed almost gone down under
the literary horizon of to-day ; but one who has
known *Blackwood* of old, can hardly wander any-
where amongst the Highlands of Scotland without
pleasant recollections of Christopher North and of
the musical bravuras of his speech.

Thomas Campbell.

Another Scotsman, who is worthy of our attention for a little time, is one of a different order ;
he is stiff, he is prim, he is almost priggish ; he is
so in his young days and he keeps so to the **very**
last.

A verse or two from one of the little poems he wrote will bring him to your memory :

> " On Linden when the sun was low,
> All bloodless lay the untrodden snow,
> And dark as winter was the flow,
> Of Iser, rolling rapidly."

And again :

> Then shook the hills with thunder riven,
> Then rushed the steed to battle driven,
> And louder than the bolts of heaven,
> Far flashed the red artillery."

If Thomas Campbell * had never written anything more than that page - long story of the "Battle of Hohenlinden," his name would have gone into all the anthologies, and his verse into all those school-books where boys for seventy years now have pounded at his martial metre in furies of declamation. And yet this bit of martial verse, so full of the breath of battle, was, at the date of its writing, rejected by the editor of a small provin-

---

* Thomas Campbell, b. 1777; d. 1844. *The Pleasures of Hope*, 1799; *Gertrude of Wyoming*, 1809; *Life of Petrarch*, 1841; Dr. Beattie's *Life*, 1850.

cial journal in Scotland — as not coming up to the true poetic standard ! *

I have spoken of Campbell as a Scotsman ; though after only a short stay in Scotland — following his university career at Glasgow — and a starveling tour upon the Continent (out of which flashed " Hohenlinden ") — he went to London ; and there or thereabout spent the greater part of the residue of a long life. He had affiliations of a certain sort with America, out of which may possibly have grown his *Gertrude of Wyoming ;* his father was for much time a merchant in Falmouth, Virginia, about 1770 ; being however a strong loyalist, he returned in 1776. A brother and an uncle of the poet became established in this country, and an American Campbell of this stock was connected by marriage with the family of Patrick Henry.

The first *coup* by which Campbell won his literary spurs, was a bright, polished poem — with its couplets all in martinet-like order — called the *Pleasures of Hope.* We all know it, if for noth-

---

* *Maclise Portrait Gallery*, London, 1883 (which cites in confirmation, *Notes and Queries*, December 13, 1862).

ing more, by reason of the sympathetic allusion
to the woes of Poland :

> " Ah, bloodiest picture in the book of time !
> Sarmatia fell, unwept, without a crime ;
> Found not a generous friend, a pitying foe,
> Strength in her arms nor mercy in her woe !
> Dropped from her nerveless grasp the shattered spear,
> Closed her bright eye and curbed her high career,
> Hope for a season bade the world farewell,
> And freedom shrieked as Kosciusko fell ! "

Even at so late a date as the death of Campbell
(1844), when they buried him in Westminster Abbey, close upon the tomb of Sheridan, some grateful Pole secured a handful of earth from the grave
of Kosciusko to throw upon the coffin of the poet.

But in addition to its glow of liberalism, this
first poem of Campbell was, measured by all the
old canons of verse, thoroughly artistic. Its
pauses, its rhymes, its longs and shorts were of the
best prize order ; even its errors in matters of fact
have an academic tinge—as, for instance, —

> "On Erie's banks, where tigers steal along ! "

The truth is, Mr. Campbell was never strong in
his natural history ; he does not scruple to put
flamingoes and palm trees into the valley of Wy-

oming. Another reason why the first poem of Campbell's, written when he was only twenty-one, came to such success, was the comparatively clear field it had. The date of publication was at the end of the century. Byron was in his boyhood; Scott had not published his *Lay of the Last Minstrel* (1805); Southey had printed only his *Joan of Arc* (1796), which few people read; the same may be said of Landor's *Gebir*, (1797); Cowper was an old story; Rogers's *Pleasures of Memory* (1792), and Moore's translation of *Anacreon* (1799–1800), were the more current things with which people who loved fresh poetry could regale themselves. The *Lyrical Ballads* of Wordsworth and Coleridge had indeed been printed, perhaps a year or two before, down in Bristol; but scarce any one read *these;* few bought them; *and yet — in that copy of the *Lyrical Ballads* was lying *perdu* — almost unknown and uncared for — the " Rime of the Ancient Mariner."

---

* De Quincey says that he was the only man in all Europe who quoted Wordsworth as early as 1802. Yet, *per contra,* the *Lyrical Ballads* had warm praises from Jeffrey (in *Monthly Review*) and from Southey (in *Critical*)—showing that the finer ears had caught the new notes from Helicon.

Gertrude of Wyoming, a poem, written at
Sydenham, near London, about 1807, and which,
sixty years ago, every good American who was
collecting books thought it necessary to place upon
his shelves, I rarely find there now. It has not the
rhetorical elaboration of Campbell's first poem;
never won its success; there are bits of war in it,
and of massacre, that are gorgeously encrimsoned,
and which are laced through and through with
sounds of fife and warwhoop; but the landscape
is a disorderly exaggeration (I have already hinted
at its palm trees) and its love-tale has only the
ardors of a stage scene in it; we know where the
tragedy is coming in, and gather up our wraps so
as to be ready when the curtain falls.

He was a born actor — in need (for his best
work) of the foot-lights, the on-lookers, the trom-
bone, the bass-drum. He never glided into victories of the pen by natural inevitable movement
of brain or heart; he stopped always and everywhere to consider his *pose.*

There is little of interest in Campbell's personal
history; he married a cousin; lived, as I said,
mostly in London, or its immediate neighborhood.

He had two sons — one dying young, and the other of weak mind — lingering many years — a great grief and source of anxiety to his father, who had the reputation of being exacting and stern in his family. He edited for a long time the *New Monthly Magazine,* and wrote much for it, but is represented to have been, in its conduct, careless, hypercritical, and dilatory. He lectured, too, before the Royal Institute on poetry; read oratorically and showily — his subject matter being semi-philosophical, with a great air of learning and academically dry; there was excellent system in his discourses, and careful thinking on themes remote from most people's thought. He wrote some historical works which are not printed nowadays; his life of Mrs. Siddons is bad; his life of Petrarch is but little better; some poems he published late in life are quite unworthy of him and are never read. Nevertheless, this prim, captious gentleman wrote many things which have the ring of truest poetry and which will be dear to the heart of England as long as English ships sail forth to battle.

A Minstrel of the Border.

Yet another Scotsman whose name will not be forgotten — whether British ships go to battle, or idle at the docks — is Walter Scott. * I scarce know how to begin to speak of him. We all know him so well — thanks to the biography of his son-in-law, Lockhart, which is almost Boswellian in its minuteness, and has dignity besides. We know — as we know about a neighbor's child — of his first struggles with illness, wrapped in a fresh sheepskin, upon the heathery hills by Smailholme Tower ; we know of the strong, alert boyhood that succeeded ; he following, with a firm seat and free rein — amongst other game — the old wives' tales and border ballads which, thrumming in his receptive ears, put the Edinboro law studies into large confusion. Swift after this comes the hurry-scurry of a boyish love-chase — beginning in Grey Friar's church-yard ;

---

* Walter Scott, b. 1771; d. 1832 ; *Lay of Last Minstrel*, 1805; *Marmion*, 1808 ; *Lady of the Lake*, 1810; *Waverley*, 1814; *Woodstock*, 1826 ; *Life of Napoleon*, 1827; *Life*, by Lockhart, 1832-37.

she, however, who sprung the race — presently
doubles upon him, and is seen no more ; and he
goes lumbering forward to another fate. It was
close upon these experiences that some friends of
his printed privately his ballad of *William and
Helen,* founded on the German Lenore :—

> " Tramp, tramp ! along the land they rode !
> Splash, splash ! along the sea !
> The scourge is red, the spur drops blood,
> The flashing pebbles flee ! "

And the spirit and dash of those four lines
were quickly recognized as marking a new power
in Scotch letters ; and an echo of them, or of their
spirit, in some shape or other, may be found, I
think, in all his succeeding poems and in all the
tumults and struggles of his life. The elder Scott
does not like this philandering with rhyme ; it will
spoil the law, and a solid profession, he thinks ;
and true enough it does. For the *Border Minstrelsy* comes spinning its delightfully musical and
tender stories shortly after Lenore ; and a little
later appears his first long poem — the *Lay
of the Last Minstrel* — which waked all Scotland and England to the melody of the new mas-

ter. He was thirty - four then ; ripening later
than Campbell, who at twenty-one had published
his *Pleasures of Hope.* There was no kinship in
the methods of the two poets ; Campbell all precision, and nice balance, delicate adjustment of
language — stepping from point to point in his
progress with all grammatic precautions and with
well-poised poetic steps and demi-volts, as studied
as a dancing master's ; while Scott dashed to his
purpose with a seeming abandonment of care, and
a swift pace that made the "pebbles fly." Just
as unlike, too, was this racing freedom of Scott's —
which dragged the mists away from the Highlands,
and splashed his colors of gray, and of the
purple of blooming heather over the moors — from
that other strain of verse, with its introspections
and deeper folded charms, which in the hands of
Wordsworth was beginning to declare itself hum-
bly and coyly, but as yet with only the rarest applause. I cannot make this distinction clearer
than by quoting a little landscape picture — let
us say from *Marmion* — and contrasting with it
another from Wordsworth, which was composed six
years or more before *Marmion* was published.

First, then, from Scott—and nothing prettier and quieter of rural sort belongs to him,—

> " November's sky is chill and drear,
>   November's leaf is red and scar;
>   Late gazing down the steepy linn
>   That hems our little garden in."

(I may remark, in passing, that this is an actual description of Scott's home surroundings at Ashestiel.)

> " Low in its dark and narrow glen
>   You scarce the rivulet might ken,
>   So thick the tangled greenwood grew,
>   So feeble trilled the streamlet through ;
>   Now, murmuring hoarse, and frequent seen
>   Through brush and briar, no longer green,
>   An angry brook it sweeps the glade,
>   Breaks over rock and wild cascade,
>   And foaming brown with double speed
>   Marries its waters to the Tweed."

There it is — a completed picture ; do what you will with it !   Reading it, is like a swift, glad stepping along the borders of the brook.

Now listen for a little to Wordsworth ; it is a scrap from Tintern Abbey :—

" Once again I see
These hedge-rows, hardly hedge-rows, little lines
Of sportive wood run wild ; these pastoral farms,
Green to the very door ; and wreaths of smoke
Sent up in silence, from among the trees !
With some uncertain notice, as might seem
Of vagrant dwellers in the houseless woods,
Or of some hermit's cave, where by his fire
The hermit sits alone."

(Here is more than the tangible picture ; the
smoke wreaths have put unseen dwellers there) ;
and again :—

"O Sylvan Wye ! thou wanderer thro' the woods,
How often has my spirit turned to thee !

        I have learned
To look on Nature, not as in the hour
Of thoughtless youth ; but hearing oftentimes
The still, sad music of humanity !
Nor harsh, nor grating, though of ample power
To chasten and subdue.   And I have felt
A presence that disturbs me with the joy
Of elevated thoughts ; a sense sublime
Of something far more deeply interfused,
Whose dwelling is the light of setting suns
And the round ocean and the living air
And the blue sky, and in the mind of men
A motion and a spirit, that impels
All thinking things, all objects of all thought,

And rolls through all things.   Therefore am I still
A lover of the meadows and the woods
And mountains."

This will emphasize the distinction, to which I would call attention, in the treatment of landscape by the two poets : Wordsworth putting *his* all on a simmer with humanities and far-reaching meditative hopes and languors ; and Scott throwing windows wide open to the sky, and saying only — look — and be glad !

In those days Wordsworth had one reader where Scott had a hundred ; and the one reader was apologetic and shy, and the hundred were loud and gushing.   I think the number of their respective readers is more evenly balanced nowadays ; and it is the readers of Scott who are beginning to be apologetic.   Indeed I have a half consciousness of putting myself on this page in that category :—As if the Homeric toss and life and play, and large sweep of rivers, and of battalions and winnowed love-notes, and clang of trumpets, and moaning of the sea, which rise and fall in the pages of the *Minstrel* and of *Marmion* — needed apology ! Apology or no, I think Scott's poems will be read for a good many years to come. The guide books and Highland travellers — and high-thoughted travellers — will keep them alive — if the critics do not; and I think you will find no better fore-reading for a trip along the Tweed or through the Trosachs than *Marmion,* and the *Lady of the Lake.*

The Waverley Dispensation.

Meantime, our author has married — a marriage, Goldwin Smith says, of "intellectual disparagement"; which I suppose means that Mrs. Scott was not learned and bookish — as she certainly was not; but she was honest, true-hearted, and domestic. Mr. Redding profanely says that she was used to plead, "Walter, my dear, you must write a new book, for I want another silk dress." I think this is apocryphal; and there is good reason to believe that she gave a little hearty home huzza at each one of Mr. Scott's quick succeeding triumphs.

Our author has also changed his home; first from the pretty little village of Lasswade, which is down by Dalkeith, to Ashestiel by the Yarrow;

IV.—5

and thence again to a farm-house, near to that un-
fortunate pile of Abbotsford, which stands on the
Tweed bank, shadowed by the trees he planted,
and shadowed yet more heavily by the story of his
misfortunes. I notice a disposition in some recent
writers to disparage this notable country home as
pseudo-Gothic and flimsy. This gives a false impression of a structure which, though it lack that
singleness of expression and subordination of
details which satisfy a professional critic, does
yet embody in a singularly interesting way, and
with solid construction, all the aspirations, tastes,
clannish vanities and archæologic whims of the
great novelist. The castellated tower is there to
carry the Scottish standard, and the cloister to
keep alive reverent memory of old religious
houses ; and the miniature Court gate, with its
warder's horn ; and the Oriole windows, whose details are, maybe, snatched from Kenilworth ; the
mass, too, is impressive and smacks all over of
Scott's personality and of the traditions he cherished.

I am tempted to introduce here some notes of a
visit made to this locality very many years ago. I

had set off on a foot-pilgrimage from the old
border town of Berwick-on-Tweed ; had kept
close along the banks of the river, seeing men
drawing nets for salmon, whose silvery scales
flashed in the morning sun. All around swept
those charming fields of Tweed-side, green with the
richest June growth ; here and there were shep-
herds at their sheep washing ; old Norham Castle
presently lifted its gray buttresses into view ; then
came the long Coldstream bridge, with its arches
shimmering in the flood below ; and after this the
palace of the Duke of Roxburgh. In thus following up leisurely the Tweed banks from Berwick,
I had slept the first night at Kelso ; had studied
the great fine bit of ruin which is there, and had
caught glimpses of Teviot-dale and of the Eildon
Hills ; had wandered out of my way for a sight of
Smailholme tower, and of Sandy Knowe — both
associated with Scott's childhood ; I passed Dryburgh, where he lies buried, and at last on an
evening of early June, 1845, a stout oarsman fer-
ried me across the Tweed and landed me in Mel-
rose.

I slept at the George Inn — dreaming (as many

a young wayfarer in those lands has since done),
of Ivanhoe and Rebecca, and border wars and *Old
Mortality*. Next morning, after a breakfast upon
trout taken from some near stream (very likely the
Yarrow or the Gala-water), I strolled two miles or
so along the road which followed the Tweed bank
upon the southern side, and by a green foot-gate
entered the Abbotsford grounds. The forest trees
—not over high at that time—were those which the
master had planted. From his favorite outdoor
seat, sheltered by a thicket of arbor-vitæ, could
be caught a glimpse of the rippled surface of the
Tweed and of the turrets of the house.

It was all very quiet — quiet in the wood-walks ;
quiet as you approached the court-yard ; the master
dead ; the family gone ; I think there was a yelp
from some young hound in an out-building, and
a twitter from some birds I did not know ; there
was the unceasing murmur of the river. Besides
these sounds, the silence was unbroken ; and when
I rang the bell at the entrance door, the jangle of
it was very startling ; startling a little terrier, too,
whose quick, sharp bark rang noisily through the
outer court.

Only an old house-keeper was in charge, who had fallen into that dreadful parrot-like way of telling visitors what things were best worth seeing — which frets one terribly. What should you or I care (fresh from *Guy Mannering* or *Kenilworth*) whether a bit of carving came from Jedburgh or Kelso ? or about the jets in the chandelier, or the way in which a Russian Grand Duke wrote his name in the visitors' book ?

But when we catch sight of the desk at which the master wrote, or of the chair in which he sat, and of his shoes and coat and cane — looking as if they might have been worn yesterday — these seem to bring us nearer to the man who has written so much to cheer and to charm the world. There was, too, a little box in the corridor, simple and iron-bound, with the line written below it, " Post will close at two." It was as if we had heard the master of the house say it. Perhaps the notice was in his handwriting (he had been active there in 1831–2 — just thirteen years before) — perhaps not ; but — somehow — more than the library, or the portrait bust, or the chatter of the well-meaning house-keeper, it brought back the

halting old gentleman in his shooting-coat, and
with ivory-headed cane — hobbling with a vigorous step along the corridor, to post in that iron-
bound box a packet — maybe a chapter of *Woodstock*.

I have spoken of the vacant house — family
gone : The young Sir Walter Scott, of the British
army, and heir to the estate — was at that date
(1845) absent in the Indies ; and only two years
thereafter died at sea on his voyage home.
Charles Scott, the only brother of the younger Sir
Walter, died in 1841.* Miss Anne Scott, the only
unmarried daughter of the author of *Waverley,*
died—worn-out with tenderest care of mother and
father, and broken-hearted — in 1833. Her only
sister, Mrs. (Sophia Scott) Lockhart, died in 1837.
Her oldest son — John Hugh, familiarly known as
"Hugh Little John "— the crippled boy, for
whom had been written the *Tales of a Grand-*

---

* He was clerk in Her Majesty's Foreign Office in London.
Carlyle says in a letter (of date of 1842), " I have the liveliest
impression of that good honest Scotch face and character,
though never in contact with the young man but once."
—Lang's *Lockhart*, p. 232, vol. ii.

father, and the darling of the two households upon
Tweed-side — died in 1831. I cannot forbear
quoting here a charming little memorial of him,
which, within the present year, has appeared in
Mr. Lang's *Life of Lockhart."*

"A figure as of one of Charles Lamb's dream-children
haunts the little beck at Chiefswood, and on that haugh at
Abbotsford, where Lockhart read the manuscript of the
Fortunes of Nigel, fancy may see 'Hugh Little John,'
'throwing stones into the burn,' for so he called the Tweed.
While children study the *Tales of a Grandfather,* he does
not want friends in this world to remember and envy the
boy who had Sir Walter to tell him stories."—P. 75,
vol. ii.

A younger son of Lockhart, Walter Scott by
name, became, at the death of the younger Walter
Scott, inheritor of all equities in the landed estate
upon Tweed-side, and the proper Laird of Abbotsford. His story is a short and a sad one; he was
utterly unworthy, and died almost unbefriended
at Versailles in January, 1853.

His father, J. G. Lockhart, acknowledging a
picture of this son, under date of 1843, in a letter
addressed to his daughter Charlotte — (later Mrs.

Hope-Scott, * and mother of the present pro-
prietress of Abbotsford), writes with a grief he
could not cover : —

"I am not sorry to have it by me, though it breaks my
heart to recall the date.   It is of the sweet, innocent, happy
boy, home for Sunday from Cowies [his school]. . . .   Oh,
God ! how soon that day became clouded, and how dark its
early close!   Well, I suppose there is another world; if not,
sure this is a blunder."

I have not spoken — because there seemed no
need to speak — of the way in which those mar-

---

* For those readers who have a failing for genealogic
quests, I give a *résumé* of the Scott family history and
succession of heirs to Abbotsford.   The earlier items are
from Scott's black-letter Bible.

Walter Scott, Senior, m. 1758 = Anne Rutherford.

Walter Scott, Bart.,
b. 1771 ; d. 1832 ; m. 1797 = Margaret Charlotte
one of twelve chil-   Carpenter, of French
dren, of whom five   blood and birth.
reached maturity.

Charlotte Sophia,   Walter, Br. Army,   Anne,   bapt.   Charles, bapt.
bapt. 1799 ;   d.   bapt. 1801 ; m.   1803 ; d. un-   1805 ; d. un-
1837 ;   m.   1820 1825, Miss Job-   m a r r i e d   married 1841.
= J. G. Lockhart.   son ; d.s.p. 1847. 1833.

John Hugh,   Walter Scott,   Charlotte, b. 1828 ; d. 1858
b. 1821 ; d.   b. 1826 ; d.   m. 1847, J. R. Hope, later
1831.   unmarried   Hope Scott.
                    1853.

Mary Monica, b. 1852 ; now Mrs. Maxwell Scott,
of Abbotsford.

vellous romantic fictions of Sir Walter came
pouring from the pen, under a cloud of mystery,
and of how the great burden of his business
embarrassments — due largely to the recklessness
of his jolly, easy-going friends, the Ballantynes
— overwhelmed him at last. Indeed, in all I
have ventured to say of Scott, I have a feeling
of its impertinence — as if I were telling you about
your next-door neighbor : we all know that swift,
brilliant, clouded career so well ! But are those
novels of his to live, and to delight coming
generations, as they have the past ? I do not
know what the very latest critics may have to
say ; but, for my own part, I have strong belief
that a century or two more will be sure to pass
over before people of discernment, and large
humanities, and of literary appreciation, will
cease to read and to enjoy such stories as that
of the *Talisman* of *Kenilworth* and of *Old Mortality*. I know 'tis objected, and with much
reason, that he wrote hastily, carelessly — that
his stories are in fact (what Carlyle called them)
extemporaneous stories. Yet, if they had been
written under other conditions, could we have

counted upon the heat and the glow which gives them illumination ?

No, no — we do not go to him for word-craft ; men of shorter imaginative range, and whose judgments wait on conventional rule, must guide us in such direction, and pose as our modellers of style. Goldsmith and Swift both may train in that company. But this master we are now considering wrote so swiftly and dashed so strongly into the current of what he had to say, that he was indifferent to methods and words, except what went to engage the reader and keep him always cognizant of his purpose. But do you say that this is the best aim of all writing ? Most surely it is wise for a writer to hold attention by what arts he can : failing of this, he fails of the best half of his intent ; but if he gains this by simple means, by directness, by limpid language, and no more of it than the thought calls for, and by such rhythmic and beguiling use of it as tempts the reader to follow, he is a safer exemplar than one who by force of genius can accomplish his aims by loose expressions and redundance of words.

Next it is objected to these old favorites of
ours, that they are not clever in the exhibit
and explication of mental processes, and their
analysis of motives is incomplete. Well, I suppose this to be true ; and that he did, to a certain
extent (as Carlyle used to allege grumblingly),
work from the outside — in. He did live in
times when men fell straightforwardly in love,
without counting the palpitations of the heart ;
and when heroes struck honest blows without
reckoning in advance upon the probable con-
tractile power of their biceps muscles. Again, it
is said that his history often lacks precision and
sureness of statement. Well, the dates are certainly sometimes twisted a few years out of their
proper lines and seasons ; but it is certain, also,
that he does give the atmosphere and the coloring
of historic periods in a completer and more
satisfying way than many much carefuller chron-
iclers, and his portraits of great historic personages are by common consent — even of the critics
— more full of the life of their subjects, and of
a realistic exhibit of their controlling character-
istics, than those of the historians proper. Noth-

ing can be more sure than that Scott was not
a man of great critical learning ; nothing is more
sure than that he was frequently at fault in
minor details ; but who will gainsay the fact that
he was among the most charming and beneficent
of story-tellers ?

There may be households which will rule him
out as old fashioned and stumbling, and wordy,
and long ; but I know of one, at least, where he
will hold his place, as among the most delightful
of visitors — and where on winter nights he will
continue to bring with him (as he has brought so
many times already) the royal figure of the Queen
Elizabeth — shining in her jewels, or sulking in
her coquetries ; and Dandie Dinmont, with his
pow-wow of Pepper and Mustard ; and King
Jamie, with Steenie and jingling Geordie ; and the
patient, prudent, excellent Jeanie Deans ; and
the weak, old, amiable mistress of Tillietudlem ;
and Rebecca, and the Lady in the Green Mantle,
and Dominie Sampson, and Peter Peebles, and Di
Vernon, and all the rest !

Glints of Royalty.

They tell us Scott loved kings : why not?
Romanticism was his nurse, from the days when
he kicked up his baby heels under the shadows of
Smailholme Tower, and Feudalism was his foster-
parent. Always he loved banners and pageantry,
and always the glitter and pomp which give their
under or over tones to his pages of balladry.
And if he stood in awe of titles and of rank, and
felt the cockles of his heart warming in contact
with these, 'twas not by reason of a vulgar tuft-
hunting spirit, nor was it due to the crass toady-
ism which seeks reflected benefit; but it grew, I
think, out of sheer mental allegiance to feudal
splendors and traditions.

Whether Scott ever personally encountered the
old king, George III., may be doubtful; but I
recall in some of his easy, family letters (perhaps
to his eldest boy Walter), most respectful and
kindly allusions to the august master of the royal
Windsor household — who ordered his home
affairs so wisely — keeping "good hours;" while,
amid the turbulences and unrest which belonged

to the American and French Revolutions — succeeding each other in portentous sequence — he
was waning toward that period of woful mental
imbecility which beset him at last, and which
clouded an earlier chapter * of our record. The
Prince Regent — afterward George IV. — was always well disposed toward Scott ; had read the
Minstrel, and *Marmion*, with the greatest grati-
fication (he did sometimes read), and told Lord
Byron as much ; even comparing the Scot with
Homer — which was as near to classicism as the
Prince often ran. But Byron, in his *English
Bards*, etc., published in his earlier days, had
made his little satiric dab at the *Minstrel* — find-
ing a lively hope in its being *the Last!*

Murray, however, in the good Christian spirit
which sometimes overtakes publishers, stanched
these wounds, and brought the poets to bask
together in the smiles of royalty. The first
Baronetcy the Prince bestowed — after coming
to Kingship — was that which made the author
of Waverley Sir Walter ; the poet had witnessed

---

* Chapter IV.   *Queen Anne and the Georges.*

and reported the scenes at the Coronation of
1820 in London ; and on the King's gala visit to
Edinboro'— when all the heights about the gray
old city boomed with welcoming cannon, and all
the streets and all the water-ways were a-flutter
with tartans and noisy with bagpipes — it was
Sir Walter who virtually marshalled the hosts,
and gave chieftain-like greeting to the Prince.
Scott's management of the whole stupendous
paraphernalia — the banquets, the processions,
the receptions, the decorations (of all which the
charming water-colors of Turner are in evidence)
— gave wonderful impressions of the masterful resources and dominating tact of the man ; now
clinking glasses (of Glenlivet) with the mellow
King (counting sixty years in that day) ; now
humoring into quietude the jealousies of Highland
chieftains ; again threading Canongate at night-
fall and afoot — from end to end — to observe if
all welcoming bannerols and legends are in place ;
again welcoming to his home, in the heat of
ceremonial occupation, the white - haired and
trembling poet Crabbe ; anon, stealing away to
his Castle Street chamber for a new chapter in

the *Peveril of the Peak* (then upon the anvil), and
in the heat, and fury, and absorption of the whole
gala business breaking out of line with a bowed
head and aching heart, to follow his best friend,
William Erskine (Lord Kinnedder), * out by
Queensferry to his burial.

It was only eight years thereafter, when this
poet manager of the great Scotch jubilee — who
seemed good for the work of a score of years —
sailed, by royal permission (an act redeeming and
glorifying royalty) upon a Government ship —
seeking shores and skies which would put new
vigor (if it might be) into a constitution broken
by toil, and into hopes that had been blighted
by blow on blow of sorrow.

Never was a royal favor more worthily be-
spoken ; never one more vainly bestowed. 'Twas
too late. No human eye — once so capable of
seeing — ever opened for a first look so wearily
upon the blue of the Mediterranean — upon the
marvellous fringed shores of lower Italy — upon

---

* Lockhart's *Life of Scott*, chapter viii., pp. 126-27,
vol. iii., Paris edition.

Rome, Florence, and the snowy Swiss portals of the Simplon.

Royalty (in person of William IV., then on the throne) asked kindly after the sick magician — who was established presently on a sick bed in London ; while the cabmen on street corners near by talked low of the " great mon " who lay there a-dying. A little show of recovery gave power to reach home — Abbotsford and Tweedside — once more. There was no hope ; but it took time for the great strength in him to waste.

Withal there was a fine glint of royalty at the end. " Be virtuous, my dear," he said to Lockhart ; " be a good man." And that utterance — the summing up of forty years of brilliant accomplishment, and of baffled ambitions — emphasized by the trembling voice of a dying man — will dwell longer in human memories, and more worthily, than the empty baronial pile we call Abbotsford, past which the scurrying waters of the Tweed ripple and murmur — as they did on the day Sir Walter was born, and on the day he was buried at Dryburgh.

IV.—6

CHAPTER III.

OUR last chapter was opened by a rather full sketch of Professor Wilson, and a briefer one of Thomas Campbell — who though of higher repute as a poet, was a far less interesting man. We then entered upon what may have seemed a very inadequate account of the great author of Waverley — because I presumed upon the reader's full and ready knowledge; and because the Minstrel's grand stride over all the Scottish country that is worth the seeing, and over all that domain in English Lands and Letters, which he made his own, has been noted by scores of tourists, and by scores of admiring commentators. You may believe me in saying — that his story was not scrimped for lack of love; indeed, it would have been easy to riot in talk about the lively drum-beat of his poems, or the

livelier and more engaging charms of his prose
Romance — through two chapters or through
ten. But we must get on ; there is a long road
before us yet.

A Start in Life.

It was somewhere about the year 1798, that a
sharp - faced, youngish Englishman — who had
been curate of a small country parish down in
Wiltshire — drove, upon a pleasant June day, on
a coach-top, into the old city of Edinboro'. This
clergyman had a young lad seated beside him,
whom he was tutoring ; and this tutoring business enabled the curate to take a respectable
house in the city. And by reason of the respectable house, and his own pleasant humor
and intelligence, he came after a year or two to
know a great many of the better folk in Edinboro', and was invited to preach an occasional
sermon at a small Episcopal chapel in his neighborhood. But all the good people he met did
not prevent his being a-hungered after a young
person whom he had left in the south of England.
So he took a vacation presently and fetched her

back, a bride, to the Scottish capital — having
(as he said) thrown all his fortune in her lap.
This fortune was of maternal inheritance, and
consisted of six well-worn silver teaspoons.
There was excellent society in Edinboro' in that
day, among the ornaments of which was Henry
Mackenzie, * a stately gentleman — a sort of dean
of the literary coteries, and the author of books
which it is well to know by name — *The Man of
Feeling* and *Julia de Roubigné* — written with
great painstaking and most exalted sentiment,
and — what we count now — much dreariness.
Then there was a Rev. Archibald Alison — he too
an Episcopal clergyman, though Scotch to the
backbone — and the author of an ingenious, but
not very pregnant book, still to be found in
old-fashioned libraries, labelled, *Alison on Taste.*
Dugald Stewart was then active, and did on one
or two occasions bring his honored presence to
the little chapel to hear the preaching of the
young English curate I spoke of. And this young
curate, poor as he is and with a young wife, has

---

* Henry Mackenzie, b. 1745; d. 1831. *Man of Feeling,*
1771; *The Lounger,* 1785.

an itch for getting into print; and does after a
little time (the actual date being 1800) publish
a booklet, which you will hardly find now, en-
titled *Six Sermons preached at Charlotte Chapel,
Edinboro, by Rev. Sydney Smith.* * But it was
not so much these sermons, as his wit and bright-
ness and great range of information, which
brought him into easy intimacy with the most
promising young men of the city. Walter Scott
he may have encountered odd whiles, though
the novelist was in those days bent on his hunt
after Border Minstrelsy, and would have been shy
of the rampant liberalism ingrained with Smith.

But the curate did meet often, and most intimately, a certain prim, delicate, short-statured,
black-eyed, smug, ambitious, precocious young
advocate named Francis Jeffrey; and it was in
a chamber of this latter — up three pair of
stairs in Buccleugh Place — that Sydney Smith,
on a certain occasion, proposed to the host and
two or three other friends there present, the establishment of a literary journal to be published

---

* Rev. Sydney Smith, b. 1771; d. 1845. *Memoir* by Lady
Holland.

quarterly; and out of that proposition grew straightway that famous *Edinburgh Review* which in its covers of buff and blue has thrived for over ninety years now — throwing its hot shot into all opposing camps of politics or of letters. I have designated two of the arch plotters, Sydney Smith and Jeffrey. Francis Horner * was another who was in at the start; he, too, a young Scotch lawyer, who went to London on the very year of the establishment of the journal, but writing for its early issues, well and abundantly. Most people know him now only by the beautiful statue of him by Chantrey, which stands in Westminster Abbey; it has a noble head, full of intellect — full of integrity. Sydney Smith said the Ten Commandments were writ all over his face. Yet the marble shows a tenderness of soul not common to those who, like him, had made a profession of politics, and entered upon a parliamentary career. But the career was short; he died in 1817 — not yet forty — leaving a reputation that was spotless; had he lived, he would have come, without a

---

* Francis Horner, b. 1778; d. 1817. *Memoirs and Correspondence*, 1843.

doubt, to the leadership of liberal opinion in England. The mourning for him was something
extraordinary in its reach, and its sincerity; a
remarkable man — whose politics never up-rooted
his affections, and whose study of the laws of
trade did not spoil his temper, or make him
abusive. His example, and his repeated advices,
in connection with the early history of the *Review*, were always against the personalities and
ugly satire which were strong features of it in the
first years, and which had their source — very
largely — in the influences and pertinacity of
another member of the *Review* Syndicate; I mean
Henry Brougham.

Henry Brougham.

This was another young lawyer — of Scottish
birth, but of Cumberland stock; ambitious like
Jeffrey and equally clever, though in a different
line; he was ungainly and lank of limb; with a
dogmatic and presuming manner, and a notice-
ably aggressive nose which became afterward the
handle (and a very good handle it made) for
those illustrative caricatures of Mr. Punch, which

lasted for a generation. Brougham * was always a debater from his boy-days — and not a little of a bully and outlaw ; precocious too — a capital Latinist — writing a paper on Optics at eighteen, which found publishment in the Philosophical Transactions ; member of the Speculative Society where Jeffrey and Mackintosh, and Alison were wont to go, and where his disputatious spirit ran riot. He didn't love to agree with anybody ; one of those men it would seem who hardly wished his dinner to agree with him.

Yet Brougham was one of the master spirits in this new enterprise, and became a great historic personage. His reputation was indeed rather political and forensic, than literary, and in his writings he inclined to scientific discussion. He had, however, a streak of purely literary ambition, and wrote a novel at one period of his life — after he had reached maturity — which he called a philosophic Romance.† Indeed this bantling was so

* Henry Brougham (Lord Brougham and Vaux), b. 1778 ; d. 1868. *Collected Speeches*, 1838. *Historic Sketches*, etc., 1839-43. Autobiography (edited by a brother), published in 1871.

† *Albert Lunel ; or The Château of Languedoc.* Lowndes

swaddled in philosophic wrappings that it could have made no noise. Very few knew of it; fewer still ever read it. He said, " It had not enough of indecency and blasphemy in it to make it popular" (it was written when Byron was in high repute). But the few who did read it thought there were other reasons for its want of success.

He drifted quickly away from Edinboro', though long keeping up his connection with the *Review;* became famous as an advocate — notably in connection with Queen Caroline's trial; went into Parliament; was eventually Lord High Chancellor, and won a place in the Peerage. He was associated intimately, too, with great beneficent schemes — such as the suppression of the slave trade, the establishment of the London University, the founding of the Society for the Diffusion of Useful Knowledge, and the urgence of the great Reform measures of 1832. Yet in all these, he arrogated more than his share of the

---

(Bohn) says — " 3 vols. post 8vo, 1844. This novel was suppressed on the eve of publication, and it is said not above five copies of the original edition are extant." The *Maclise Portrait Gallery* speaks of an issue in 1872.

honor, wearying his associates by incessant bicker-
ing and scolding, picking flaws in everything not
entirely his own ; jealous, suspicious, conceited to
the last degree ; never generous in praise of one
living beside him ; an enormous worker, with
sinews of iron, and on occasions (which are of record) speaking and wrangling in the House of
Commons until two of the morning, and then going home — not to sleep — but to write a thirty-
page article for the *Edinburgh Review*. Such men
make a place for themselves, and keep it. He
was an acrid debater, but a most thorough one —
holding all aspects of a case in view ; never getting muddled ; ready with facts ; ready with fal-
lacies (if needed) ; ready for all and any interrup-
tions ; setting them on fire by the stress of his
argumentation — like carbons in an electric cir-
cuit ; ready with storms of irony and running
into rough-edged sarcasm with singular ease and
sharpest appetite.

On a May evening of 1845 the present writer had
the pleasure of watching him for an hour or more
in the House of Lords. He was lank, as I have
said ; awkward, nervous, restless ; twisting the

great seals at his watch-chain; intent upon everything; now and then sniffing the air, like a terrier
that has lost the scent; presenting a petition, in
the course of the session, in favor of some Newfoundland clients who were anxious for more direct
postal communication — who objected that their
mails were sent in a roundabout way *via* Halifax.
Whereupon Lord Stanley (afterward Earl Derby),
then Secretary for the Colonies, rose in explanation, "regretting that his Lordship had not com-
municated with the Colonial Office, which had
considered the question raised; there was no communication by land; the harbor was often closed
by ice; therefore present methods were followed,"
etc. All of which was set forth with most charming grace and suavity; but Lord Stanley was no
sooner ended than the irascible Scotch peer, net-
tled, as would seem, by the very graciousness of
the explanation, was upon his feet in an instant,
with a sharp "M' Lards," that promised fun;
and thereafter came a fusillade of keenest, ironi-
cal speech — thanking the honorable Secretary for
"the vera impartant information, that as St.
John's was upon an island, there could be no com-

munication by land; and perhaps his learned *Lardship* supposes, with an acumen commensurate with his *great* geographic knowledge, that the sending of the mails by the way of Halifax will have a tendency to *thaw* the ice in the Harbor of St. John's," and so on, for a ten minute's storm of satiric and witty banter. And then — an awkward plunge backward into his seat — a new, nervous twirling of his watch-seals, a curious smile of self-approval, followed by a lapse into the old nervous unrest.

There was no serenity in Brougham — no repose — scarce any dignity. His petulance and angry sarcasm and frequent ill-nature made him a much hated man in his latter days, and involved him in abusive tirades, which people were slow to forgive.

Francis Jeffrey.

As for Mr. Jeffrey, his associate on the *Review*, and for many years its responsible editor, he was a very different man — of easy address, courteous, gentlemanly — quite a master of deportment. Yet it was he who ripped open with his critical knife Southey's *Thalaba* and the early

poems of Wordsworth. But even his victims
forgot his severities in his pleasantly magnetic
presence and under the caressing suavities of his
manner. He was brisk, *débonnaire*, cheery — a
famous talker ; not given to anecdotes or story-
telling, but bubbling over with engaging book-
lore and poetic hypotheses, and eager to put
them into those beautiful shapes of language
which came — as easily as water flows — to his
pen or to his tongue. He said harsh things, not
for love of harsh things ; but because what provoked them grated on his tastes, or his sense of
what was due to Belles Lettres. One did not —
after conversing with him — recall great special
aptness of remark or of epithet, so much as the
charmingly even flow of apposite and illustrative
language — void of all extravagances and of all
wickednesses, too. Lord Cockburn says of his
conversation : —

"The listeners' pleasure was enhanced by the personal
littleness of the speaker. A large man [Jeffrey was very
small] could scarcely have thrown off Jeffrey's conversational flowers without exposing himself to ridicule. But
the liveliness of the deep thoughts and the flow of bright expressions that animated his talk, seemed so natural and

appropriate to the figure that uttered them, that they were
heard with something of the delight with which the slender-
ness of the trembling throat and the quivering of the wings
make us enjoy the strength and clearness of the notes of a
little bird." *

The first Mrs. Jeffrey dying early in life, he
married for second wife a very charming American lady, Miss Wilkes;† having found time —
notwithstanding his engrossment with the *Review*
— for an American journey, at the end of which
he carried home his bride. Some of his letters
to his wife's kindred in America are very delightful — setting forth the new scenes to which the
young wife had been transported. He knew just
what to say and what not to say, to make his
pictures perfect. The trees, the church-towers,
the mists, the mosses on walls, the gray heather —
all come into them, under a touch that is as light
as a feather, and as sharp as a diamond.

---

* *Life and Correspondence of Lord Jeffrey*, by Lord Cockburn, p. 283, vol. i., Harper's edition.

† A grandniece of the great marplot John Wilkes of
George III.'s time, and a near connection (if I am not mistaken) of Captain Wilkes of the South Sea Expedition and of
the Mason and Slidell seizure.

His honors in his profession of advocate grew, and he came by courtesy to the title of Lord Jeffrey — (not to be confounded with that other murderous Lord Jeffreys, who was judicial hangman for James II.). He is in Parliament too; never an orator properly; but what he says, always clean cut, sensible, picturesque, flowing smoothly — but rather over the surface of things than into their depths. Accomplished is the word to apply to him; accomplished largely and variously, and with all his accomplishments perfectly in hand.

Those two hundred papers which he wrote in the *Edinburgh Review* are of the widest range — charmingly and piquantly written. Yet they do not hold place among great and popular essays; not with Macaulay, or Mackintosh, or Carlyle, or even Hazlitt. He was French in his literary aptitudes and qualities; never heavy; touching things, as we have said, with a feather's point, yet touching them none the less surely.

Could he have written a book to live? His friends all thought it, and urged him thereto. He thought not. There would be great toil, he said, and mortification at the end; so he lies buried, where we leave him, under a great tumulus of most happy *Review* writing.

Sydney Smith.

I return now to the clever English curate who was the first to propose the establishment of that great Northern *Review,* out of which Lord Jeffrey grew. Smith had written very much and well, and had cracked his jokes in a way to be heard by all the good people of Edinboro'. But he was poor, and his wife poor; he had his fortune to make; and plainly was not making it there, tutoring his one pupil. So, in 1804, he struck out for London, to carve his way to fortune. He knew few there; but his clever papers in the *Review* gave him introduction to Whig circles, and a social plant, which he never forfeited. Lord and Lady Holland greatly befriended him; and he early came to a place at the hospitable board of that famous Holland House — of whose green quietudes we have had glimpses, in connection with Addison, and in connection with Charles Fox — and whose mistress in the days we are now upon, showed immense liking for the brilliant and witty parson.

All this while, the Rev. Sydney was seeking preaching chances; but was eyed doubtfully by those who had pulpits in their gift. He was too independent — too witty — too radical — too hateful of religious conventionalisms — too *Edinburgh Reviewish.* Neither was he a great orator; rather scornful of explosive clap-trap or of noisy pulpit rhetoric; yet he had a resonant voice — earnest in every note and trill; often sparkling to his points in piquant, conversational way, but wanting quick-witted ones for their reception and comprehension. He lacked too, in a measure — what is another great resource for a preacher — the unction which comes of deep, sustained, devotional feeling, and a conviction of the unmatchable importance and efficacy of sacerdotal influences. I think there was no time in his life when he would not rather beguile a wayward soul by giving him a good, bright witticism to digest than by exhibit of the terrors of the Law. His Gospel — by preference — was an intellectual gospel; yet not one that reposed on creeds and formulas. His

7

heart was large, and his tolerance full. He was a proud Churchman indeed, and loved to score dissenters; but delighted in the crack of his witticisms, more than he mourned over their apostasy. Among the "evening meetings" that he knew very much of, and specially relished, were those at his own little homestead, with closed blinds, and a few friends, and hot-water, and — lemons!

I do not at all mean to imply that he had habits of dissipation, or was ever guilty of vulgar excesses. Of all such he had a wholesome horror; but along with it, he had a strong and abiding fondness for what he counted the good things of life, and the bright things, and the play of wit, and the encounter of scholarly weapons.

One beautiful priestly quality, however, always shone in him: that was his kindliness for the poor and feeble — his sympathy with them — his working for their benefit; and though he trusted little in appeals to the mere emotional nature, yet in his charity sermons he drew such vivid pictures of the suffering poor folk who had come under his eye, as to put half his auditors in tears.

His preaching in London at this early period

was for the most part at an out-of-the-way chapel,
in connection with a Foundling Hospital; but he
gave a series of Philosophic Lectures at the Royal
Institution — never reckoned by himself with his
good work — which were besieged by people who
came to enjoy his witty sayings. In a few years,
however, he secured a valuable church gift in
Yorkshire, where he built a rectory — the ugliest
and "honest-est house" in the county — and entertained London and Scottish friends there, and
grew to enjoy — much as he could — the trees,
flowers, and lawns which he planted, and with
which he coquetted, though only in a half-hearted
way. His supreme love was for cities and crowds;
he counting the country at its best only a kind
of "healthy grave"; flowers, turf, birds are very
well in their way, he says, but not worth an hour
of the rational conversation only to be had
where a million are gathered in one spot. *

And he does at last come to the million—getting, after his Whig friends came into power, and
after the Reform revolution was over, the royal

---

* Cited from recollection; but very close to his own utterance, in a letter to a friend.

appointment to a canonry in connection with St. Paul's Cathedral.*

He also has the gift of a new country "living" in Somersetshire, where he passes his later summer in another delightfully equipped home ; and between these two church holdings, and certain legacies conveniently falling due, he has a large income at command, and enjoys it, and makes the poor of his parishes enjoy it too.

He has taken a lusty hand in that passage of the Reform bill (1832), and while its success seemed still to be threatened by the sullen opposition of the House of Lords, he made that famous witty comparison in which he likened the popular interest in Reform to a great storm and tide which had set in from the Atlantic, and the opposition of the Lords, to the efforts of Dame Partington, who lived upon the beach, and —

"who was seen at the door of her house with mops and pattens, trundling her mop, squeezing out the sea-water, and

---

* This was arranged through Lord Grey, in exchange for a place in Bristol Cathedral, which had been bestowed by his Tory friend Lyndhurst. To the same friend he was indebted for his living at Combe Fleurey.

vigorously pushing away the Atlantic Ocean. The Atlantic was roused. Mrs. Partington's spirit was up. But I need not tell you the contest was unequal. The Atlantic Ocean beat Mrs. Partington. She was excellent at a slop or a puddle, but she should not have meddled with a tempest."

And this happy and droll comparison was met with a great roar of laughter and of applause that ran all over England. The same tactics of witty ridicule belonged also to his attacks upon Tractarianism and Puseyism, which made stir in his latter days. Indeed, his bump of veneration was very small ; and his drollery creeps into his letters as into his speech. He writes of a visit to Edinboro':

"My old friends were glad to see me ; some were turned Methodists, some had lost their teeth, some had grown very fat, some were dying, and, alas ! many were dead. But the world is a coarse enough place; so I talked away, comforted some, praised others, kissed some old ladies, and passed a very riotous week." *

He writes to Moore, the poet :

"DEAR MOORE : I have a breakfast of philosophers at ten, punctually, to-morrow—'muffins and metaphysics, crumpets and contradiction.' Will you come ? "

---

* *Life and Times of Rev. Sydney Smith*, by STUART J. REID, p. 226, 1885.

When Mrs. Smith is ailing at her new home in Somersetshire he says :

"Mrs. S—— has eight distinct illnesses, and I have nine. We take something every hour, and pass the mixture between us."

One part of his suffering comes of hay fever, as to which he says :

"Light, dust, contradiction — the sight of a dissenter — anything sets me sneezing ; and if I begin sneezing at twelve, I don't leave off till two, and am heard distinctly in Taunton (when the wind sets that way), a distance of six miles."

This does not show quite so large a reserve and continence of speech as we naturally look for in the clerical profession ; but this, and other such do, I think, set the Rev. Sydney Smith before us, with his witty proclivities, and his unreserve, and his spirit of frolic, as no citations from his moral and intellectual philosophy could ever do. And I easily figure to myself this portly, well-preserved gentleman of St. Paul's, fighting the weaknesses of the gout with a gold-headed cane, and picking his way of an afternoon along the pavements of Picca-dilly, with eye as bright as a bird's, and beak as sharp as a bird's — regaling himself with the thought of the dinner for which he is booked, and of the brilliant talkers he is to encounter, with the old parry and thrust, at Rogers's rooms, or under the noble ceiling of Holland House.

A Highlander.

Another writer — whose sympathies from the beginning were with the Liberalism of the *Edinburgh Review* (though not a contributor till some years after its establishment) was Sir James Mackintosh.* A Highlander by birth — he was at Aberdeen University — afterwards in Edinboro', where he studied medicine, and getting his Doctorate, set up in London — eking out a support, which his medical practice did not bring, by writing for the papers.

This was at the date when the recent French Revolution and its issues were at the top of all men's thoughts; and when Burke had just set up his glittering bulwark of eloquence and of sentiment in his famous "Reflections"; and

---

* James Mackintosh, b. 1765; d. 1832; *Vindiciæ Gallicæ* (reply to Burke), 1791 ; *Memoirs*, by his son, 1835.

our young Doctor (Mackintosh) — full of a bumptious Whiggism, undertook a reply to the great statesman — a reply so shrewd, so well-seasoned, so sound — that it brought to the young Scotchman (scarce twenty-five in those days) a fame he never outlived. It secured him the acquaintance of Fox and Sheridan, and the friendship of Burke, who in his latter days invited the young pamphleteer, who had so strongly, yet respectfully, antagonized his views, to pass a Christmas with him at his home of Beaconsfield. Of course, such a success broke up the doctoring business, and launched Mackintosh upon a new career. He devoted himself to politics; was some time an accredited lecturer upon the law of nations; was knighted presently and sent to Bombay on civil service. His friends hoped he might find financial equipment there, but this hope was vain; red-tape was an abomination to him always; cash-book and ledger represented unknown quantities; he knew no difference between a shilling and a pound, till he came to spend them. He was in straits all his life.

His friendship for Jeffrey, Sydney Smith, and

Brougham was maintained by correspondence, and on his return from India he became an occasional contributor to the great Scotch *Review* on various subjects.

His range of acquirements was most wide — too wide and too unceasing for the persistency which goes with great single achievements. His histories are fragments. His speeches are misplaced treatises; his treatises are epitomes of didactic systems. When we weigh his known worth, his keenness of intellect, his sound judgment, his wealth of language, his love for thoroughness — which led him to remotest sources of information — his amazing power in colloquial discourse, we are astonished at the little store of good things he has left. There was a lack in him, indeed, of the salient and electrical wit of Sydney Smith; a lack of the easy and graceful volubility of Jeffrey; lack of the abounding and illuminating rhetoric of Macaulay; but a greater lack was of that dogged, persistent working habit which gave to Brougham his triumphs.

Yet Mackintosh was always plotting great literary designs; but his fastidious taste, and his critical hunger for all certainties, kept him forever in the search of new material and appliances. He was dilatory to the last degree; his caution always multiplied delays; no general was ever so watchful of his commissariat — none ever so unready for a "Forward, march!" Among his forecasts was that of a great history of England. Madame de Staël urged her friend to take possession of her villa on Lake Geneva and, like Gibbon, write his way there to a great fame. He did for awhile set himself resolutely to a beginning at the country home of Weedon Lodge in Buckinghamshire — accumulated piles of fortifying MSS. and private records; but for outcome we have only that clumsy torso which outlines the Revolution of 1688.*

His plans wanted a hundred working years, instead of the thirty which are only allotted to men. What Jeffrey left behind him marks, I think, the full limit of his powers; the same is true of Brougham, and true probably of Macaulay; and I think no tension and no incentive would have

---

* *History of the Revolution in England in 1688, Comprising a View of the Reign of James II. from his Accession to the Enterprise [sic] of the Prince of Orange,* London, 1834.

wrought upon Sydney Smith to work greater and
brighter things than he did accomplish. A bishopric would only have set his gibes into coruscа-
tion at greater tables, and perhaps given larger
system to his charities. But Mackintosh never
worked up to the full level of his best power and
large learning, except in moments of conversational exaltation.

Rest at Cannes.

Before closing our chapter we take one more
swift glimpse at that arch-plotter for Whiggism —
in the early days of the *Edinburgh Review* —
whom we left fidgetting in the House of Lords,
on a May evening of 1845. He had a longer life
by far than most of those who conspired for the
maintenance of the great blue and buff forerunner of British critical journals. He was only
twenty-three when he put his shoulder to the
quarterly revolutions of the *Edinburgh* — youngest of all the immediate founders ;* and he out-

---

* Smith, Jeffrey, Brown, Horner, and Brougham. Ste-
phens : *Hours in a Library*, iii., 140.

The "Brown" alluded to as one of the founders, was Dr.
Thomas Brown, a distinguished physician and psychologist

lived them all and outvoiced them all in the
hurly-burly of the world.

He survived Macaulay too — an early contributor of whom we shall have more to say — and
though he was past eighty at the death of the
historian, he was alert still, and his brain va-
grantly active ; but the days of his early glory and
fame — when the young blusterer bolstered up
Reform, and slew the giants of musty privilege
and sent "the schoolmaster abroad," and antagonized slavery, were gone ; * so, too, were those

---

(b. 1778; d. 1820), who after issue of third number of the
Review, had differences with Jeffrey (virtual editor) which
led him to withdraw his support. *Life*, by Welsh, p. 79
et seq.

* I cannot forbear giving — though only in a note — one
burst of his fervid oratory, when his powers were at their
best :

"It was the boast of Augustus — it formed part of the
glare in which the perfidies of his earlier years were lost —
that he found Rome of brick, and left it of marble — a praise
not unworthy of a great prince, and to which the present
reign [George IV.] has its claim also.   But how much nobler
will be our Sovereign's boast, when he shall have it to say,
that he found law dear and left it cheap; found it a sealed
book, and left it a living letter; found it the patrimony of
the rich, left it the inheritance of the poor; found it the

palmy times when he made the courts at Westminster ring with his championship of that poor Queen (who, whatever her demerits — and they were many — was certainly abominably maltreated by a husband far worse than she) ; times when the populace who espoused her cause shouted bravos to Harry Brougham — times when he was the best known and most admired man in England ; all these, and his chancellorship, and his wordy triumphs in the House of Lords, were far behind him, and the inevitable loss of place and power fretted him grievously. He quarrelled with old coadjutors ; in Parliament he shifted from bench to bench ; in the weakness of age, he truckled to power ; he exasperated his friends, and for years together — his scoldings, his tergiversations, and his plaid trousers made a mine of mockery for Mr. Punch. As early as 1835-40, Lord Brougham had purchased an estate in the south of France, in a beautiful nook of that mountain shore which sweeps eastward from the neighborhood of Mar-

---

two-edged sword of craft and oppression, left it the staff of honesty and the shield of innocence." Speech, on *Present State of the Law*, February 7, 1828.

seilles — along the Mediterranean, and which so many travellers now know by the delights of the Cornice Road and Monaco, and Mentone, and San Remo. The little fishing village where years ago Lord Brougham set up his Villa of Louise Eléonore (after a darling and lost child) is now a suburb of the fashionable resort of Cannes. At his home there, amongst the olives, the oleanders and the orange-trees, the disappointed and petulant ex-chancellor passed most of the later years of his life.

Friends dropping in upon him — much doubting of their reception — found him as the humors changed, peevish with strong regrets and recriminations, or placid under the weight of his years, and perhaps narcotized by the marvellous beauty of the scenes around him.

He was over ninety at his death in 1868. To the very last, a man not to be reckoned on : some days as calm as the sea that rippled under his window ; other days full of his old unrest and petulancies. There are such men in all times and in all societies—sagacious, fussy, vain, indefatigable, immensely serviceable, cantankerous ;

we *can't* get on without them; we are for ever wishing that we could.

In our next chapter we shall come upon a critic, who was a famous editor — adroit, strong, waspish, bookish, and ignoble. We shall encounter a king, too — of whom we have thus far only had glimpses — who was jolly — excellently limbed and conditioned physically — a man "of an infinite jest," too, and yet as arrant a dastard — by all old-fashioned moral measures of character — as Falstaff himself. Again we shall follow traces of a great poet — but never a favorite one — who has left markings of his career, strong and deep; a man who had a Greek's delight in things of beauty, and a Greek's subtlety of touch; but one can fancy a faun's ears showing their tips upon his massive head, and (without fancy) grow conscious of a heathenism clouding his great culture. Other two poets of lighter mould we shall meet; — more gracious, lighter pinioned — prettily flitting — iridescent — grace and sparkle in their utterances, but leaving no strong markings "upon the sands of time."

CHAPTER IV.

WE have wandered much in our two last chapters beyond what may be reckoned strictly English lands, into that pleasant region lying between the Tweed and the Firth of Forth; and it was north of the heights of Lammermuir and of the Pentland Hills, and in that delightful old city which is dominated by the lesser heights of the Salisbury crags, the Castle Rock, and Calton Hill, that we found the builders of that great *Review,* which in its livery of buff and blue still carries its original name. I traced the several careers of Sydney Smith, Lord Brougham, and Judge Jeffrey; the first of these, from a humble village curacy, coming to be one of the most respected literary men of England, and an important official of St. Paul's Cathedral; if his wit had been less lively he might have risen to a bishopric. Brougham was, first, essayist, then advocate, then Parliamentary orator, then Reformer, then Lord High Chancellor — purging the courts of much legal trumpery — always a scold and quarreller, and gaining in the first year of William IV. his barony of Brougham and Vaux : hence the little squib of verse, which will help to keep his exact title in mind :

> " Why is Lord Brougham like a sweeping man
>   That close by the pavement walks?
>   Because when he's done all the sweep that he can
>   He takes up his *Broom* and *Valks !* "

As for Jeffrey, he became by his resolute industry and his literary graces and aptitudes one of the most admired and honored critics of Great Britain.

Gifford and His Quarterly.

Our start-point to-day is on the Thames — in that devouring city of London, which very early in the century was laying its tentacles of growth on all the greenness that lay between Blackwall and Bayswater, and which — athwart the Thames shores — strode blightingly from Clapham to Hackney.

It was, I believe, in the year 1809 that Mr. John Murray, the great publisher of London — stirred, perhaps, by some incentive talk of Walter Scott, or of other good Tory penmen, and emulous of the success which had attended Jeffrey's *Review* in the north, established a rival one—called simply *The Quarterly* — intended to represent the Tory interests as unflinchingly and aggressively as the *Edinburgh* had done Whig interests. The first editor was a William Gifford * (a name worth remembering among those of British critics), who was born in Devonshire. He was the son of a dissolute house-painter, and went to sea in his young

---

* William Gifford, b. 1757; d. 1826. I give the birth-date named by himself in his autobiography, though the new *National Dictionary of Biography* gives date of 1756. Gifford — though not always the best authority — ought to have known the year when he was born.

Ed. *Quarterly Review*, 1809-1824; *Juvenal*, 1802; *Ben Jonson*, 1816.

Some interesting matter concerning the early life of Gifford may be found in Memoirs of *John Murray*, vol. 1, pp. 127 *et seq*.

days, but was afterwards apprenticed to a shoe-
maker. Some piquant rhymes he made in those
days attracting the attention of benevolent gentlemen, he was put in the way of schooling, and at
Oxford, where he studied. It was while there he
meditated, and perhaps executed, some of those
clever translations from Persius and Juvenal,
which he published somewhat later. He edited
Ben Jonson's works in a clumsy and disputatious
way, and in some of his earlier, crude, satirical
rhymes (*Baviad*) paid his respects to Madame
Thrale in this fashion :

> "See Thrale's gay widow with a satchel roam,
> And bring in pomp laborious nothings home."

Again he pounces upon the biographer of Dr.
Johnson thus-wise :

> "Boswell, aping with preposterous pride,
> Johnson's worst frailties, rolls from side to side,
> His heavy head from hour to hour erects,
> Affects the fool, and is what he affects."

These lines afford a very good measure of his
poetic grace and aptitude; but they give only a

remote idea of his wonderful capacity for abusing people who did not think as he thought. He had a genius in this direction, which could not have discredited an editorial room in New York — or elsewhere. Walter Scott — a warm political friend — speaks of him as "a little man, dumpled up together, and so ill-made as to seem almost deformed;" and I think that kindly gentleman was disposed to attribute much of the critic's rancor to his invalidism; but if we measure his printed bile in this way, there must be credited him not only his usual rheumatic twinges, but a pretty constant dyspepsia, if not a chronic neuralgia. Of a certainty he was a most malignant type of British party critics; and it is curious how the savors of its first bitterness do still linger about the pages of the *Quarterly Review.*

John Wilson Croker * will be best known to our readers as the editor of that edition of Boswell's

---

* John Wilson Croker, b. 1780; d. 1857, wrote voluminously for the *Quarterly Review; Life of Johnson* (ed.), 1831; his *Memoirs* and *Correspondence,* 1885.

"Johnson," to which I have alluded. Within the last ten years, however, his memoirs and correspondence, in two bulky volumes, have excited a certain languid interest, and given entertainment to those who are curious in respect to the political wire-pullings of the early part of this century in London. He was an ardent co-worker with Gifford in the early history of the *Quarterly Review*. He loved a lord every whit as well as Gifford, and by dint of a gentlemanly manner and gentlemanly associations was not limited to the "back-stairs way" of Mr. Gifford in courting those in authority. His correspondence with dukes and earls — to all of whom he is a "dear Croker" — abound; and his account of interviews with the Prince Regent, and of dinners at the Pavilion in Brighton, are quite Boswellian in their particularity and in their atmosphere of worship. There is also long account in the book to which I have called attention, of a private discourse by George IV., of which Mr. Croker was sole auditor; and it is hard to determine whether Croker is more elated by having the discourse to record, or Mr. Jennings by having such a record to edit.

A Prince Regent.

This royal mention brings us once more, for a little space, to our background of kings. Of the old monarch, George III., we have had frequent and full glimpses. We wish to know something now of that new prince (whom we saw in our Scott chapter), but who in 1810, when his father's faculties failed altogether, became Regent; and we wish to learn what qualities are in him and under what training they developed.

The old father had a substructure of good, hard sense that showed itself through all his obstinacies; for instance, when Dr. Markham, who was appointed tutor to his two oldest sons — Prince of Wales and Duke of York — asked how he should treat them, the old king said : "Treat them ? Why, to be sure, as you would any gentleman's sons ! If they need the birch, give them the birch, as you would have done at Westminster." But when they had advanced a bit, and a certain Dr. Arnold (a later tutor) undertook the same regimen, the two princes put their forces together and gave the doctor such a drubbing that he never tried birch again. But it was always a very close life the princes led in their young days; the old king was very rigorous in respect of hours and being out at night. By reason of which George IV. looked sharply after his opportunities, when they did come, and made up for that early cloister-hood by a large laxity of regimen.* Indeed, he opened upon a very glittering career of dissipations — the old father groaning and grumbling and squabbling against it vainly.

It was somewhere about 1788 or 1789, just when the French Revolution was beginning to throw its bloody foam over the tops of the Bastille, that temporary insanity in the old King George III. did for a very brief space bring the Prince into consequence as Regent. Of the happening of this, and of the gloom in the palace, there is story in the diary of Madame D'Arblay,† who was her-

---

* Very much piquant talk about George IV. and his friends may be found in the *Journal of Mary Frampton from 1779 until 1846.* London: Sampson Low & Co., 1885.

† *English Lands and Letters,* vol. iii., pp. 168–70.

self in attendance upon the Queen. If, indeed,
George III. had stayed mad from that date, and
the Prince — then in his fullest vigor, and a great
friend of Fox and other Liberal leaders — had
come to the full and uninterrupted responsibility
of the Regency, his career might have been very
different. But the old king rallied, and for
twenty years thereafter put his obstinacies and
Tory caution in the way of the Prince, who, with
no political royalties to engage him, and no important official duties (though he tried hard to
secure military command), ran riot in the old way.
He lavishes money on Carlton House; builds
a palace for Mrs. Fitzherbert; coquets with
Lady Jersey; affects the fine gentleman. No
man in London was prouder of his walk, his cane,
his club nonchalance, his taste in meats, his
knowledge of wines, ragoûts, indelicate songs, and
arts of the toilette. Withal, he is well-made, tall,
of most graceful address, a capital story-teller,
too; an indefatigable diner-out; a very fashion-
plate in dress — corsetted, puffed out in the chest
like a pouter pigeon; all the while running vigorously and scandalously in debt, while the

father is setting himself squarely against any further parliamentary grant in his favor. There are, however — or will be — relentings in the old King's mind, if "Wales" will promise to settle down in life and marry his cousin, Caroline of Brunswick — if, indeed, he be not already married to Mrs. Fitzherbert, which some avow and some deny. It does not appear that the Prince is very positive in his declarations on this point — yes or no. So he filially yields and accedes to a marriage, which by the conditions of the bargain is to bring him £70,000 to pay his debts withal. She is twenty-seven — a good-looking, spirited Brunswicker woman, who sets herself to speaking English — nips in the bud some love-passages she has at home, and comes over to conquer the Prince's affections — which she finds it a very hard thing to do. He is polite, however ; is agreeably disposed to the marriage scheme, which finds exploitation with a great flourish of trumpets in the Chapel Royal of St. James. The old King is delighted with his niece ; the old Queen is a little cool, knowing that the Prince does not care a penny for the bride, and believing that she ought to have found that out.

She does find it out, however, in good time; and finds out about Mrs. Fitzherbert and her fine house; and does give her Prince some very severe curtain lectures — beginning early in that branch of wifely duty. The Prince takes it in dudgeon; and the dudgeon grows bigger and bigger on both sides (as such things will); finally, a year or more later — after the birth of her daughter, the Princess Charlotte — proposals for separation are passed between them (with a great flourish of diplomacy and golden sticks), and accepted with exceeding cordiality on both sides.

Thereafter, the Prince becomes again a man about town — very much about town indeed. Everybody in London knows his great bulk, his fine waistcoats, his horses, his hats and his wonderful bows, which are made with a grace that seems in itself to confer knighthood. For very many years his domestic life, — what little there was of it, — passed without weighty distractions. His Regency when established (1811) was held through a very important period of British history; those great waves of Continental war which ended in Waterloo belonged to it; so did the American war of 1812; so did grave disaffections and discontent at home. He did not quarrel with his cabinets, or impede their action; he learned how to yield, and how to conciliate. Were it only for this, 'tis hardly fair to count him a mere posture-master and a dandy.

He loved, too, and always respected his old mother, the Queen of George III.;* loved too, — in a way — and more than any other creature in the world except himself, that darling daughter of his, the Princess Charlotte, who at seventeen became the bride of Leopold, afterward King of Belgium, — she surviving the marriage only a year. Her memory is kept alive by the gorgeous marble cenotaph you will see in St. George's Chapel, Windsor.

It was only when George IV. actually ascended the throne in 1820 that his separated wife put in a disturbing appearance again; she had been living very independently for some years on the Con-

---

* Queen Charlotte, d. 1818.

tinent; and it occurred to her — now that George
was actually King — that it would be a good thing,
and not impinge on the old domestic frigidities, to
share in some of the drawing-room splendors and
royalties of the British capital.   To George IV. it
seemed very awkward ; so it did to his cabinet.
Hence came about those measures for a divorce,
and the famous trial of Queen Caroline, in which
Brougham won oratorical fame by his brilliant
plea for the Queen.   This was so far successful as
to make the ministerial divorce scheme a failure ;
but the poor Queen came out of the trial very
much bedraggled ; whether her Continental life
had indeed its criminalities or not, we shall never
positively know.   Surely no poor creature was
ever more sinned against than she, in being whee-
dled into a match with such an unregenerate par-
taker in all deviltries as George IV.   But she was
not of the order of women out of which are made
martyrs for conscience's sake.   It was in the
year 1821 that death came to her relief, and her
shroud at last whitened a memory that had
stains.

A Scholar and Poet.

We freshen the air now with quite another presence. Yet I am to speak of a man whose life was full of tumult, and whose work was full of learning and power — sometimes touched with infinite delicacy.

He was born four years after Sydney Smith and Walter Scott — both of whom he survived many years; indeed he lacked only eleven years of completing a century when he died in Florence, where most of his active — or rather inactive — life was passed. I allude to the poet and essayist, Walter Savage Landor. * He is not what is called a favorite author; he never was; he never will be. In fact, he had such scorn of popular applause, that if it had ever happened to him in moments of dalliance with the Muses, and of frolic with rhythmic language, to set such music afloat as the world would have repeated and loved to repeat, I think he would have torn the music out in disdain for

---

* W. S. Landor, b. 1775; d. 1864. *Gebir*, 1798; *Imaginary Conversations*, 1824; Foster's *Life*, 1869.

the approval of a multitude. Hear what he says, in one of his later poetic utterances : —

" Never was I impatient to receive
　What *any* man could give me.　When a friend
　Gave me my due, I took it, and no more,
　Serenely glad, because that friend was pleased.
　I seek not many ; many seek not me.
　If there are few now seated at my board,
　I pull no children's hair because they munch
　Gilt gingerbread, the figured and the sweet,
　Or wallow in the innocence of whey ;
　Give *me* wild boar, the buck's broad haunch give *me*,
　And wine that time has mellowed, even as time
　Mellows the warrior hermit in his cell." *

Such verse does not invite a large following, nor did the man. Pugnacious, tyrannic, loud-mouthed, setting the world's and the Church's rubrics at defiance ; yet weighing language to the last jot and tittle of its significance, and — odd-whiles — putting little tendernesses of thought and far-reaching poetic aspirations into such cinctures of polished verse — so jewelled, so compact, so classic, so fine — that their music will last and be admired as long, I think, as English speech

---

* P. 465.　*Last Fruit from an Old Tree.*

lasts. Apart from all this man wrote, there is a strange, half-tragic interest in his life, which will warrant me in telling you more of him than I have told of many whose books are more prized by you.

He was the son of a Dr. Landor, of Warwick, in middle England, who by reason of two adroit marriages was a man of fortune, and so secured eventually a very full purse to the poet, who if he had depended only on the sale of his literary wares, would have starved. Language was always young Landor's hobby; and he came, by dint of good schooling, to such dexterity in the use of Latin, as to write it in verse or prose with nearly the same ease as English. He loved out-of-door pursuits in boyhood and all his life; was greatly accomplished, his biographer says, in fishing — especially with a cast-net; and of the prey that sometimes came into such net there is this frolicsome record :

> " In youth 'twas there I used to scare
> A whirring bird, or scampering hare,
> And leave my book within a nook
> Where alders lean above the brook,

To walk beyond the third mill-pond
And meet a maiden fair and fond
Expecting me beneath a tree
Of shade for two, but not for three.
Ah, my old Yew, far out of view,
Why must I bid you both adieu?" *

At Oxford he was a marked man for his cleverness and for his audacities; these last brought
him to grief there, and going home upon his
rustication, he quarrelled with his father. Thereafter we find him in London, where he publishes
his first little booklet of poems (1795); only
twenty then; counted a fierce radical; detesting
old George III. with his whole heart; admiring
the rebel George Washington and declaring it;
loving the French, too, with their liberty and
fraternity song, until it was silenced by the
cannonading of Napoleon; thenceforward, he
counts that people a nation of "monkeys, fit only
to be chained."

But Landor never loved London. We find him
presently wandering by the shores of Wales, and
among its mountains. Doubtless he takes his

---

* Colvin cites this from unpublished verses.

cast-net with him; the names of Ianthé and
Ioné decorate occasional verses; a certain Rose
Aylmer he encounters, too, who loans him a book
(by Clara Reeve), from a sketch in which he
takes hint for his wild, weird poem of *Gebir*, his
first long poem — known to very few — perhaps
not worth the knowing. It is blind in its drift;
war and pomp and passion in it — ending with a
poisoned cup; and contrasting with these, such
rural beatitudes as may be conjured under Afric
skies, with tender love-breezes, ending in other
beatitudes in coral palaces beneath the sea. This,
at any rate, is the phantasmic outline which a
reading leaves upon my own memory. Perhaps
another reader may be happier.

That shadowy Rose Aylmer, through whom the
suggestion for the poem came, was the real daughter of Lord Aylmer, of the near Welsh country;
what Landor's intimacy with her may have been, in
its promise or its reach, we do not know; but we
do know that when she died, somewhat later and
in a far country, the poet gave her name embalm-
ment in those wonderful little verses, which poor
Charles Lamb, it is said, in his later days, would

IV.—9

repeat over and over and over, never tiring of the
melody and the pathos.   Here they are :—

> " Ah, what avails the sceptred race,
>   Ah, what the form divine !
> What — every virtue, every grace !
>   Rose Aylmer, all were thine.
> Rose Aylmer, whom these wakeful eyes
>   May weep, but never see,
> A night of memories and of sighs
>   I consecrate to thee ! "

Meantime, growing into a tempestuous love for
the wild Welsh country, he bargains for a great
estate, far up in a valley which opens down upon
the larger valley in which lies Abergavenny ; and
being rich now by reason of his father's death,
parts with his beautiful ancestral properties in the
Warwickshire region, lavishing a large portion
of the sales-money upon the savagery of the new
estate in Wales.   He plants, he builds, he plays
the monarch in those solitudes.   He marries, too,
while this mountain passion is on him, a young
girl of French or Swiss extraction — led like a
lamb into the lion's grasp.   But the first Welsh
quarrel of this poet-monarch — who was severely

classic, and who fed himself all his life through on the thunder-bolts of Jupiter — was with his neighbors ; next with his workmen ; then with his tenants ; then the magistrates ; last with every-body ; and in a passion of disgust, he throws down his walls, turns astray his cattle, lets loose his mountain tarns, and leaving behind him the weltering wreck of his half-built home, goes over with his wife to Jersey, off the coast of Normandy. There she, poor, tired, frighted, worried bird — maybe with a little of the falcon in her — would stay ; *he* would not. So he dashes on inconti-nently — deserting her, and planting himself in mid-France at the old city of Tours, where he de-votes himself to study.

This first family tiff, however, gets its healing, and — his wife joining him — they go to Como, where Southey (1817) paid them a visit ; this poet had been one of the first and few admirers of *Gebir,* which fact softened the way to very much of mutual and somewhat over-strained praises between these two.* From Como Landor went to

---

* In his *Last Fruits from an Old Tree,* p. 334, Moxon Edition, Landor writes : "Southey could grasp great subjects

Pisa — afterward to Florence, his home thenceforth
for very many years ; first in the town proper and
then in a villa at Fiesole from which is seen that
wondrous view — none can forget who have beheld
it — of the valley, which seems a plain — of the
nestling city, with its great Brunelleschi dome,
its arrow-straight belfry of Giotto, its quaint tower
of the Palazzo Vecchio, its cypress sentinels on the
Boboli heights, its River Arno shining and winding, and stealing away seaward from the amphithe-
atre of hills — on whose slopes are dotted white
convents, sleeping in the sun, and villas peeping
out from their cloakings of verdure, and the gray
shimmer of olive orchards.

Landor in Italy.

It was in Florence that Landor wrote the greater
part of those *Imaginary Conversations* which have
given him his chief fame ; but which, very possibly, may be outlived in the popular mind by the
wonderful finish and the Saxon force which belong
to many of his verselets.

and master them ; Coleridge never attempted them ; Wordsworth attempted it and failed." This is strongly *ex parte !*

The conversations are just what their name implies — the talk of learned, or distinguished men, on such topics as they were supposed to be most familiar with; all *imagined*, and set forth by the brain of Landor, who took a strange delight in thus playing with the souls of other men and making them the puppets of his will. One meets in his pages Roger Ascham and Lady Jane Grey, Milton and Andrew Marvel, and Achilles and Helena; then we are transported from Mount Ida to the scene of a homely colloquy between Washington and Franklin — about monarchy and Republicanism. Again we have Leofric and Godiva telling their old story with a touching dramatic interest; and can listen — if we will — to long and dullish dispute between Dr. Johnson and Horne Tooke, about Language and its Laws; from this — in which Landor was always much interested — we slip to the Philo-Russianism of a talk between Peter the Great and Alexis. There are seven great volumes of it all — which must belong to all considerable libraries, private or other, and which are apt to keep very fresh and uncut. Of course there is no logical continuity

—no full exposition of a creed, or a faith, or a philosophy. It is a great, wide, eloquent, homely jumble; one bounces from rock to rock, or from puddle to puddle (for there are puddles) at the will of this great giant driver of the chariot of imaginary talk.* There are beauties of expression that fascinate one; there are sentences so big with meaning as to bring you to sudden pause; there are wearisome chapters about the balance of French verselets, in which he sets up the poor Abbé Delille on rhetorical stilts— only to pelt him down; there are page-long blotches of crude humor, and irrelevant muddy tales, that you wish were out. As sample of his manner, I give one or two passages at random. Speaking of Boileau, he says :—

"In Boileau there is really more of diffuseness than of brevity [he loves thus to slap a popular belief straight in the face]; few observe this, because [Boileau] abounds in short sentences; and few are aware that sentences may be very short, and the writer very prolix; as half a dozen

---

* I would strongly urge, however, the reading and purchase, if may be, of Colvin's charming little *Golden Treasury* collection from Landor.

stones rising out of a brook give the passenger more trouble
than a plank across it." [He abounds in short, pert similes
of this sort which seem almost to carry an argument in
them.]

[Again] "Caligula spoke justly and admirably when he
compared the sentences of Seneca *to sand without lime.*"

[And once more] "He must be a bad writer, or, however,
a very indifferent one, to whom there are no inequalities.
The plants of such table-land are diminutive and never
worth gathering. . . . The vigorous mind has mountains to climb and valleys to repose in. Is there any sea
without its shoal? On that which the poet navigates, he
rises intrepidly as the waves riot around him, and sits com-
posedly as they subside. . . ."

"Level the Alps one with another, and where is their
sublimity? Raise up the Vale of Tempe to the downs
above, and where are those sylvan creeks and harbors in
which the imagination watches while the soul reposes, those
recesses in which the gods partook of the weaknesses of
mortals, and mortals the enjoyments of the gods."

The great learning of Landor and his vast information, taken in connection with his habits of
self-indulgence (often of indolence), assure us
that he must have had the rare talent, and the
valuable one, of riddling books — that is, of skim-
ming over them — with such wonderfully quick
exercise of wit and judgment as to segregate the
valuable from the valueless parts. 'Tis not a bad

quality ; nor is it necessarily (as many suppose) attended by superficiality. The superficial man does indeed skim things ; but he pounces as squarely and surely upon the bad as upon the good ; he works by mechanical process and progression — here a sentence and there a sentence ; but the man who can race through a book well (as did Dr. Johnson and Landor), carries to the work — in his own genius for observation and quick discernment — a chemical mordant that bites and shows warning effervescence, and a signal to stay, only where there is something strong to bite.

Landor's Domesticities.

Meanwhile, we have a sorry story to tell of Landor's home belongings. There is a storm brewing in that beautiful villa of Fiesole. Children have been born to the house, and he pets them, fondles them — seems to love them absorbingly. Little notelets which pass when they are away, at Naples, at Rome, are full of pleasantest paternal banter and yearning. But those children have run wild and are as vagrant as the winds.

The home compass has no fixed bearings and

points all awry — the mother, never having sympathy with the work which had tasked Landor in
those latter years, has, too, her own outside vanities and a persistent petulance, which breaks out
into rasping speech when Jupiter flings his thun-
derbolts. So Landor, in a strong rage of determination, breaks away : turns his back on wife and
children — providing for them, however, gener-
ously — and goes to live again at Bath, in England.

For twenty-three years he stays there, away
from his family (remembering, perhaps, in self-
exculpating way, how Shakespeare had once done
much the same), rambling over his old haunts,
writing new verse, revamping old books, petting
his Pomeranian dog, entertaining admiring guests,
fuming and raving when crossed. He was more
dangerously loud, too, than of old ; and at last is
driven away, to escape punishment for some scathing libels into which a storm of what he counted
righteous rage has betrayed him. It must have
been a pitiful thing to see this old, white-haired
man — past eighty now — homeless, as good as
childless, skulking, as it were, in London, just

before sailing for the Continent, — appearing suddenly at Forster's house, seated upon his bed there, with Dickens in presence, mumbling about Latin poetry and its flavors !

He finds his way to Genoa, then to Florence, then to the Fiesole Villa once more ; but it would seem as if there were no glad greetings on either side ; and in a few days estrangement comes again, and he returns to Florence.   Twice or thrice more those visits to Fiesole are repeated, in the vague hope, it would seem, floating in the old man's mind, that by some miracle of heaven, aspects would change there — or perhaps in him — and black grow white, and gloom sail away under some new blessed gale from Araby.   But it does never come; nor ever the muddied waters of that home upon the Florentine hills flow pure and bright again.

Final Exile and Death.

He goes back — eighty-five now — toothless, and trembling under weight of years and wranglings, to the Via Nunziatina, in Florence ; he has no means now — having despoiled himself for the

benefit of those living at his Villa of Fiesole, who
will not live with him, or he with them; he is
largely dependent upon a brother in England.
He passes a summer, in these times, with the
American sculptor Story. He receives occasional
wandering friends; has a new pet of a dog to
fondle.

There is always a trail of worshipping women
and poetasters about him to the very last; but the
bad odor of his Bath troubles has followed him;
Normanby, the British Minister, will give him no
recognition; but there is no bending, no flinching
in this great, astute, imperious, headstrong, ill-
balanced creature. Indeed, he carries now under
his shock of white hair, and in his tottering figure,
a stock of that coarse virility which has distinguished him always — which for so many has its
charm, and which it is hard to reconcile with the
tender things of which he was capable; — for instance, that interview of Agamemnon and Iphigenia — so cunningly, delicately, and so feelingly
told — as if the story were all his own, and had no
Greek root — other than what found hold in the
greensward of English Warwickshire. And I

close our talk of Landor, by citing this : Iphigenia
has heard her doom (you know the story) ; she
must die by the hands of the priest — or, the
ships, on which her father's hopes and his fortunes
rest, cannot sail.   Yet, she pleads ; — there may
have been mistakes in interpreting the cruel ora-
cle, — there may be hope still, —

" The Father placed his cheek upon her head
And tears dropt down it; but, the king of men
Replied not :   Then the maiden spoke once more, —
'O, Father, says't thou nothing ?   Hear'st thou not
Me, whom thou ever hast, until this hour,
Listened to — fondly ; and awakened me
To hear my voice amid the voice of birds
When it was inarticulate as theirs,
And the down deadened it within the nest.'
He moved her gently from him, silent still :
And this, and this alone, brought tears from her
Although she saw fate nearer : then, with sighs, —
'I thought to have laid down my hair before
Benignant Artemis, and not have dimmed
Her polisht altar with my virgin blood ;
I thought to have selected the white flowers
To please the Nymphs, and to have asked of each
By name, and with no sorrowful regret,
Whether, since both my parents willed the change,
I might at Hymen's feet bend my clipt brow,
And — (after those who mind us girls the most)

Adore our own Athena, that she would
Regard me mildly with her azure eyes;
But — Father! to see you no more, and see
Your love, O Father! go, ere I am gone.'
Gently he moved her off, and drew her back,
Bending his lofty head far over hers,
And the dark depths of nature heaved and burst:
He turned away : not far, but silent still :
She now first shuddered; for in him — so nigh,
So long a silence seemed the approach of death
And like it.   Once again, she raised her voice,—
' O Father! if the ships are now detained
And all your vows move not the Gods above
When the knife strikes me, there will be one prayer
The less to them; and, purer can there be
Any, or more fervent, than the daughter's prayer
For her dear father's safety and success?'
A groan that shook him, shook not his Resolve.
An aged man now entered, and without
One word, stept slowly on, and took the wrist
Of the pale maiden. She looked up and saw
The fillet of the priest, and calm cold eyes:
Then turned she, where her parent stood and cried,—
' O, Father! grieve no more! the ships can sail!' ' "

When we think of Landor, let us forget his
wrangles — forget his wild impetuosities — forget
his coarsenesses, and his sad, lonely death ; and —
instead — keep in mind, if we can, that sweet
picture I have given you.

Prose of Leigh Hunt.

It was some two years before George IV. came
to the Regency, and at nearly the same date
with the establishment of Murray's *Quarterly,*
that Mr. Leigh Hunt,* in company with his
brother John Hunt, set up a paper called the
Examiner — associated in later days with the
strong names of Fonblanque and Forster. This
paper was of a stiffly Whiggish and radical sort,
and very out-spoken — so that when George IV.,
as Regent, seemed to turn his back on old Whig
friends, and show favors to the Tories (as he did),
Mr. Leigh Hunt wrote such sneering and abusive
articles about the Regent that he was prose-
cuted, fined, and clapped into prison, where he
stayed two years. They were lucky two years
for him — making reputation for his paper and
for himself; his friends and family dressed up
his prison room with flowers (he loved overmuch

---

* Leigh Hunt, b. 1784; d. 1859. *Francesca da Rimini,*
1816; *Recollections of Byron,* 1828; *The Indicator,* 1819–21;
Autobiography, 1850.

little luxuries of that sort); Byron, Moore, Godwin, and the rest all came to see him ; and there
he caught the first faint breezes of that popular
applause which blew upon him in a desultory and
rather languid way for a good many years afterward — not wholly forsaking him when he had
grown white-haired, and had brought his delicate,
fine, but somewhat feeble pen into the modern
courts of criticism.

I do not suppose that anybody in our day goes
into raptures over the writings of Leigh Hunt;
nevertheless, we must bring him upon our record
— all the more since there was American blood in
him. His father, Isaac Hunt, was born in the Bar-
badoes, and studied in Philadelphia; in the latter
city, Dr. Franklin and Tom Paine used to be
visitors at his grandfather's house. At the out-
break of the Revolution, Hunt's father, who —
notwithstanding his Philadelphia wife — was a
bitter loyalist, went to England — his departure
very much quickened by some threats of punish-
ing his aggressive Toryism. He appears in England as a clergyman — ultimately wedded to
Unitarian doctrines; finding his way sometimes

to the studio of Benjamin West — talking over
Pennsylvania affairs with that famous artist, and
encountering there, as it chanced, John Trumbull, a student in painting — who in after years
bequeathed an art-gallery to Yale College. It
happens, too, that this Colonel Trumbull, in 1812,
when the American war was in progress, was
suspected as a spy, and escaped grief mainly by
the intervention of Isaac Hunt.

The young Hunt began early to write — finding
his way into journalism of all sorts ; his name associated sooner or later with *The News,* and dramatic critiques ; with the *Examiner,* the *Reflector,*
the *Indicator,* the *Companion,* and the *Liberal* —
for which latter he dragged his family down into
Italy at the instance of Byron or Shelley, or both.
That *Liberal* was intended to astonish people and
make the welkin ring ; but the Italian muddle
was a bad one, the *Liberal* going under, and
an ugly quarrel setting in ; Hunt revenging himself afterward by writing *Lord Byron and his
Contemporaries,* — a book he ultimately regretted :
he was never strong enough to make his bitterness respected. Honeyed words became him

better; and these he dealt out — wave upon wave — on all sorts of unimportant themes. Thus, he writes upon "Sticks"; and again upon "Maid-servants"; again on "Bees and Butterflies" (which is indeed very pretty); and again "Upon getting up of a cold morning"—in which he compassionates those who are haled out of their beds by "harpy-footed furies"—discourses on his own experience and sees his own breath rolling forth like smoke from a chimney, and the windows frosted over.

"Then the servant comes in: 'It is very cold this morning, is it not?' 'Very cold, sir.' 'Very cold, indeed, isn't it?' 'Very cold, indeed, sir.' 'More than usually so, isn't it, even for this weather?' 'Why, sir, I think it *is*, sir.' . . . And then the hot water comes: 'And is it quite hot? And isn't it too hot?' And what 'an unnecessary and villainous custom this is of shaving.'"

Whereupon he glides off, in words that flow as easily as water from a roof — into a disquisition upon flowing beards — instancing Cardinal Bembo and Michelangelo, Plato and the Turks. Listen again to what he has to say in his *Indicator* upon "A Coach":—

IV.—10

"It is full of cushions and comfort; elegantly colored inside and out; rich yet neat; light and rapid, yet substantial. The horses seem proud to draw it. The fat and fair-wigged coachman lends his sounding lash, his arm only in action, and that but little; his body well set with its own weight. The footman, in the pride of his nonchalance, holding by the straps behind, and glancing down sideways betwixt his cocked hat and neckcloth, standing swinging from East to West upon his springy toes. The horses rush along amidst their glancing harness. Spotted dogs leap about them, barking with a princely superfluity of noise. The hammer cloth trembles through all its fringe. The paint flashes in the sun."

Nothing can be finer — if one likes that sort of fineness. We follow such a writer with no sense of his having addressed our intellectual nature, but rather with a sense of pleasurable regalement to our nostrils by some high wordy perfume.

Hawthorne, in *Our Old Home*, I think, tells us that even to extreme age, the boyishness of the man's nature shone through and made Hunt's speech like the chirp of a bird; he never tired of gathering his pretty roses of words. It is hard to think of such a man doing serious service in the rôle of radical journalist — as if he *could* speak dangerous things! And yet, who can tell? They say Robespierre delighted in satin facings to his coat, and was never without his *boutonnière*.

We all know the figure of Harold Skimpole, in Dickens's *Bleak House*, with traits so true to Leigh Hunt's, that the latter's friends held up a warning finger, and said : " For shame ! " to the novelist. Indeed, I think Dickens felt relentings in his later years, and would have retouched the portrait ; but a man who paints with flesh and blood pigments cannot retouch.

Certain it is that the household of Hunt was of a ram-shackle sort, and he and his always very much out at ends. Even Carlyle, who was a neighbor at Chelsea, was taken aback at the easy way in which Hunt confronted the butcher-and-baker side of life ; and the kindly Mrs. Carlyle drops a half-querulous mention of her shortened larder and the periodic borrowings of the excellent Mrs. Hunt.

Hunt's Verse.

But over all this we stretch a veil now, woven out of the little poems that he has left. He wrote no great poems, to be sure ; for here, as in

his prose, he is earnestly bent on carving little
baskets out of cherry-stones — little figures on
cherry-stones — dainty hieroglyphics, but always
on cherry-stones !

His "Rimini," embodying that old Dantesque
story about Giovanni and Paolo and Francesca, is
his longest poem. There are exceedingly pretty
and delicate passages in it ; I quote one or two :

> " For leafy was the road with tall array
>   On either side of mulberry and bay,
>   And distant snatches of blue hills between;
>   And there the alder was, with its bright green,
>   And the broad chestnut, and the poplar's shoot
>   That, like a feather, waves from head to foot;
>   With ever and anon majestic pines;
>   And still, from tree to tree, the early vines
>   Hung, garlanding the way in amber lines.
>
>   .   .   .   .   .   .
>
>   And then perhaps you entered upon shades,
>   Pillowed with dells and uplands 'twixt the glades
>   Through which the distant palace, now and then,
>   Looked forth with many windowed ken—
>   A land of trees which, reaching round about,
>   In shady blessing stretched their old arms out
>   With spots of sunny opening, and with nooks
>   To lie and read in — sloping into brooks,
>   Where at her drink you started the slim deer,
>   Retreating lightly with a lovely fear.

And all about the birds kept leafy house,
And sung and sparkled in and out the boughs,
And all about a lovely sky of blue
Clearly was .felt, or down the leaves laughed through."

And so on — executed with ever so much of delicacy —but not a sign or a symbol of the grave and melancholy tone which should equip, even to the utmost hem of its descriptive passages, that tragic story of Dante.

Those deft, little feathery touches — about deer, and birds, and leafy houses, are not scored with the seriousness which in every line and pause should be married with the intensity of the story. The painting of Mr. Watts, of the dead Francesca — ghastly though it be — has more in it to float one out into the awful current of Dante's story than a world of the happy wordy meshes of Mr. Hunt. A greater master would have brought in, maybe, all those natural beauties of the landscape — the woods, the fountains, the clear heaven — but they would all have been toned down to the low, tragic movement, which threatens, and creeps on and on, and which dims even the blue sky with forecast of its controlling gloom.

There is no such inaptness or inadequacy where
Leigh Hunt writes of crickets and grasshoppers
and musical boxes. In his version of the old classic
story of "Hero and Leander," however, the impertinence (if I may be pardoned the language) of
his dainty wordy dexterities is even more strik-
ingly apparent. *His* Hero, waiting for her Leander, beside the Hellespont,

> "Tries some work, forgets it, and thinks on,
>   Wishing with perfect love the time were gone,
>   And lost to the green trees with their sweet singers,
>   Taps on the casement-ledge with idle fingers."

No — this is not a Greek maiden listening for
the surge of the water before the stalwart swimmer of Abydos; it is a London girl, whom the
poet has seen in a second-story back window, med-
itating what color she shall put to the trimming
of her Sunday gown!

Far better and more beautiful is this fathoming
of the very souls of the flowers :

> " We are the sweet Flowers ,
>   Born of sunny showers,
>   Think, whene'er you see us, what our beauty saith :
>   Utterance mute and bright,
>   Of some unknown delight,
>   We feel the air with pleasure, by our simple breath ;

All who see us, love us;
We befit all places;
Unto sorrow we give smiles; and unto graces, graces.

' Mark our ways—how noiseless
All, and sweetly voiceless,
Though the March winds pipe to make our passage clear;
Not a whisper tells
Where our small seed dwells,
Nor is known the moment green, when our tips appear.
We tread the earth in silence,
In silence build our bowers,
And leaf by leaf in silence show, 'till we laugh atop, sweet
Flowers!

.   .   .   .

" Who shall say that flowers
Dress not Heaven's own bowers?
Who its love, without them, can fancy — or sweet floor?
Who shall even dare
To say we sprang not there,
And came not down that Love might bring one piece of
heav'n the more?
Oh, pray believe that angels
From those blue Dominions
Brought us in their white laps down, 'twixt their golden
pinions."

No poet of this — or many a generation past —
has said a sweeter or more haunting word for the
flowers.

We will not forget the " Abou-ben-Adhem ;" nor

shall its commonness forbid our setting this charmingly treated Oriental fable, at the end of our mention of Hunt — a memorial banderole of verse : —

"Abou Ben Adhem (may his tribe increase!)
    Awoke one night from a deep dream of peace,
    And saw within the moonlight in his room,
    Making it rich and like a lily in bloom,
    An Angel, writing in a book of gold.
    Exceeding peace had made Ben Adhem bold;
    And to the presence in the room, he said, —
    'What writest thou?' The Vision raised its head,
    And with a look made of all sweet accord
    Answered, 'The names of those who love the Lord.'
    'And is mine one?' said Abou. 'Nay, not so;'
    Replied the Angel. Abou spoke more low,
    But cheerly still; and said, 'I pray thee, then,
    Write me as one that loves his fellow-men.'
    The Angel wrote and vanished. The next night
    It came again, with a great wakening light,
    And showed the names whom love of God had blessed,
    And lo! — Ben Adhem's name led all the rest!'"

An Irish Poet.

Among those who paid their visits of condolence to Leigh Hunt in the days of his prisonhood, was Moore* the author of *Lalla Rookh* and of *The Loves of the Angels*. He was not used to paying visits in such quarters, for he had an instinctive dislike for all uncanny things and disagreeable places ; nor was he ever a great friend of Hunt; but he must have had a good deal of sympathy with him in that attack upon the Prince Regent which brought about Hunt's conviction. Moore, too, had his gibes at the Prince — thinking that great gentleman had been altogether too neglectful of the dignities of his high estate ; but he was very careful that his gibes should be so modulated as not to put their author in danger.

Lalla Rookh may be little read nowadays; but not many years have passed since this poem and others of the author's used to get into the finest of bindings, and have great currency for bridal and birth-day gifts. Indeed, there is a witching melody in Moore's Eastern tales, and a delightful shimmer and glitter of language, which none but the most cunning of our present craftmasters in verse could reach.

---

* Thomas Moore, b. 1779 ; d. 1852. *Lalla Rookh*, 1817. *Life of Byron*, 1830. *Alciphron*, 1839.

Moore was born in Dublin, his father having kept a wine-shop there ; and his mother (he tells us) was always anxious about the quality of his companions, and eager to build up his social standing — an anxiety which was grafted upon the poet himself, and which made him one of the wariest, and most coy and successful of society-seekers — all his life.

He was at the Dublin University—took easily to languages, and began spinning off some of *Anacreon's* numbers into graceful English, even before he went up to London — on his old mother's savings — to study law at the Temple. He was charmingly presentable in those days ; very small, to be sure, but natty, courteous, with a pretty modesty, and a voice that bubbled over into music whenever he recited one of his engaging snatches of melody. He has letters to Lords, too, and the most winning of tender speeches and smiles for great ladies. He comes to an early interview with the Prince of Wales — who rather likes the graceful Irish singer, and flatters him by accepting the dedication of *Anacreon* with smiles of condescension — which

Mr. Moore perhaps counted too largely upon. Never had a young literary fellow of humble birth a better launch upon London society. His Lords' letters, and his pretty conciliatory ways, get him a place of value (when scarce twenty-four) in Bermuda. But he is not the man to lose his hold on London; so he goes over seas only to put a deputy in place, and then, with a swift run through our Atlantic cities, is back again. It is rather interesting to read now what the young poet says of us in those green days :—In Philadelphia, it appears, the people quite ran after him :

"I was much caressed while there. . . . and two or three little poems, of a very flattering kind, some of their choicest men addressed to me." [And again.] "Philadelphia is the only place in America which can boast any literary society." [Boston people, I believe, never admired Moore overmuch.]

Here again is a bit from his diary at Ballston — which was the Saratoga of that day :—

"There were about four hundred people — all stowed in a miserable boarding-house. They were astonished at our asking for basons and towels in our rooms; and thought we might condescend to come down to the Public Wash, with the other gentlemen, in the morning."

Poor, dainty, Moore! But he is all right when he comes back to London, and gives himself to old occupations of drawing-room service, and to the coining of new, and certainly very sweet and tender, Irish melodies. He loved to be tapped on the shoulder by great Dowagers, sparkling in diamonds, and to be entreated — "Now, dear Mr. Moore, *do* sing us one more song."

And it was pretty sure to come : he delighted in giving his very feeling and musical voice range over the heads of fine-feathered women. The peacock's plumes, the shiver of the crystal, the glitter of Babylon, always charmed him.

Nor was it all only tinkling sound that he gave back. For proof I cite one or two bits :—

"Then I sing the wild song, 'twas once such a pleasure to
    hear,
When our voices commingling breathed, like one, on the ear;
And, as Echo far off thro' the vale, my sad orison rolls,
I think, O my love! 'tis thy voice from the Kingdom of Souls
Faintly answering still the notes that once were so dear."

And again :—

" Dear Harp of my Country! farewell to thy numbers,
    This sweet wreath of song is the last we shall twine.

Go sleep, with the Sunshine of Fame on thy slumbers,
  Till touched by some hand less unworthy than mine.

" If the pulse of the patriot, soldier, or lover
  Have throbbed at our lay, 'tis thy glory alone;
I was *but* as the wind, passing heedlessly over,
  And all the wild sweetness I wak'd was thy own."

This is better than dynamite to stir Ireland's best pulses, even now.

Lalla Rookh.

Mr. Moore had his little country vacations — among them, that notable stay up in the lovely county of Derbyshire, near to Ashbourne and Dovedale, and the old fishing grounds of Walton and of Cotton — where he wrote the larger part of his first considerable poem, *Lalla Rookh* — which had amazing success, and brought to its author the sum of £3,000. But I do not think that what inspiration is in it came to him from the hollows or the heights of Derbyshire; I should rather trace its pretty Oriental confusion of sound and scenes to the jingle of London chandeliers. Yet the web, the gossamer, the veils and

the flying feet do not seem to touch ground any-
where in England, but shift and change and grow
out of his Eastern readings and dreams.

Moore married at thirty-two — after he was
known for the Irish melodies, but before the publication of *Lalla Rookh ;* and in his *Letters and
Diary* (if you read them — though they make an
enormous mass to read, and frighten most people
away by their bulk), you will come upon very frequent, and very tender mention of "Dear Bessie"
— the wife.   It is true, there were rumors that he
wofully neglected her, but hardly well founded.
Doubtless there was many a day and many a week
when she was guarding the cottage and the children
at Sloperton ; and he bowing and pirouetting his
way amongst the trailing robes of their ladyships
who loved music and literature in London ; but
how should he refuse the invitations of his Lordship this or that ?   Or how should she — who
has no robes that will stand alone — bring her
pretty home gowns into that blazon of the salons ?
Always, too (if his letters may be trusted), he is
eager to make his escape between whiles — wearied
of this *tintamarre*—and to rush away to his cot-

tage at Sloperton* for a little slippered ease, and a romp with the children. Poor children — they all drop away, one by one — two only reaching maturity — then dying. The pathetic stories of the sickening, the danger and the hush, come poignantly into his Diary, and it does seem that the winning clatter of the world gets a hold upon his wrenched heart over-quickly again. But what right have you or I to judge in such matters ?

There are chirrupy little men — and women, too, — on whom grief does not seem to take a hard grip ; all the better for them ! Moore, I think, was such a one, and was braced up always and everywhere by his own healthy pulses, and, perhaps, by a sense of his own sufficiency. His vanities are not only elastic, but — by his own bland and child-like admissions — they seem sometimes almost monumental. He writes in his *Diary*,

---

* Sloperton was near the centre of Wiltshire, a little way northward from the old market-town of Devizes. Mr. William Winter, in his *Gray Days and Gold*, has given a very charming account of this home of Moore's and of its neighborhood — so full of English atmosphere, and of the graces and benignities of the Irish poet, as to make me think regretfully of my tamer mention.

"Shiel (that's an Irish friend) says I am the first poet of the day, and join the beauty of the Bird-of-Paradise's plumes to the strength of the eagle's wing." Fancy a man copying that sort of thing into his own *Diary,* and regaling himself with it!

Yet he is full of good feeling — does not cherish resentments — lets who will pat him on the shoulder (though he prefers a lord's pat). Then he forgives injuries or slights grandly; was once so out with Jeffrey that a duel nearly came of it; but afterward was his hail-fellow and good friend for years. Sometimes he shows a magnanimous strain — far more than his artificialities of make-up would seem to promise. Thus, being at issue with the publisher, John Murray (a long-dated difference), he determines on good advisement to be away with it; and so goes smack into the den of the great publisher and gives him his hand : such action balances a great deal of namby-pambyism.

But what surprises more than all about Moore, is the very great reputation that he had in his day. We, in these latter times, have come to reckon him (rather rashly, perhaps) only an arch gossipper of letters — a butterfly of those metro-

politan gardens — easy, affable, witty, full of
smiles, full of good feeling, full of pretty little
rhythmical utterances — singing songs as easy as a
sky-lark (and leaving the sky thereafter as empty) ;
planting nothing that lifts great growth, or tells
larger tale than lies in his own lively tintinnabu-
lation of words.

Yet Byron said of him : " There is nothing
Moore may not do, if he sets about it." Sydney
Smith called him " A gentleman of small stature,
but full of genius, and a steady friend of all that
is honorable." Leigh Hunt says : "I never received a visit from him, but I felt as if I had been
talking with Prior or Sir Charles Sedley." It is
certain that he must have been a most charming
companion. Walter Scott says : " It would be a
delightful addition to life if Thomas Moore had a
cottage within two miles of me." Indeed, he was
always quick to scent anything that might amuse,
and to store it up. His diaries overflow with
these bright specks and bits of talk, which may
kindle a laugh, but do not nestle in the memory.

But considered as a poet whose longish work
ought to live and charm the coming generations,

IV.—11

his reputation certai..ly does not hold to the old illuminated heights. Poems of half a century ago, which *Lalla Rookh* easily outshone, have now put the pretty orientalisms into shade. Nor can we understand how so many did, and do, put such twain of verse-makers as Byron and Moore into one leash, as if they were fellows in power. In the comparison the author of the *Loves of the Angels* seems to me only a little important-looking, kindly pug — nicely combed, with ribbons about the neck — in an embroidered blanket, with jingling bells at its corners; and Byron — beside him — a lithe, supple leopard, with a tread that threatens and a dangerous glitter in the eye. Milk diet might sate that other; but this one, if occasion served, would lap blood.

In the pages that follow we shall, among others, more or less notable, encounter again that lithe leopard in some of his wanton leaps — into verse, into marriage, into exile, and into the pit of death at Missolonghi.

CHAPTER V.

WE opened our budget in the last chapter with the *Quarterly Review*, which was just getting upon its legs through the smart, keen, and hard writing of Mr. William Gifford. It throve afterward under the coddling of the most literary of the Tory gentlemen in London, and its title has always been associated with the names of John Wilson Croker, of Dr. Southey, and of Mr. Lockhart. It is a journal, too, which has always been tied by golden bonds to the worship of tradition and of vested privilege, and which has always been ready with its petulant, impatient bark of detraction at reform or reformers, or at any books which may have had a scent of Liberalism. Leigh Hunt, of course, came in for periodic scathings — some of them deserved ; some not deserved. Indeed, I am half-

disposed to repent what may have seemed a too
flippant mention of this very graceful poet and
essayist. Of a surety, there is an abounding afflu-
ence of easy language — gushing and disporting
over his pages — which lures one into reading and
into dreamy acquiescence ; but read as much as
we may, and as long as we will, we shall go away
from the reading with a certain annoyance that
there is so little to keep out of it all — so little
that sticks to the ribs and helps.

As for the poet Moore, of whom also we may
have spoken in terms which may seem of too great
disparagement to those who have loved to linger
in his

> " Vale of Cashmere
> With its roses, the brightest that earth ever gave.
> Its temples, and grottos, and fountains as clear
> As the love-lighted eyes that hang over their wave,"

no matter what may become of these brilliant
orientalisms, or of his life of Byron, or of his
diaries, and his " Two-penny Post Bag," it is certain that his name will be gratefully kept alive by
his sparkling, patriotic, and most musical Irish

melodies; and under that sufficient monument we leave him.

As for Landor — surely the pages in which we dealt with him were not too long: a strange, strong bit of manhood — as of one fed on collops of bear's meat; a big animal nature, yet wonderfully transfused by a vivid intellectuality — fine and high — that pierced weighty subjects to their core; and yet — and yet, singing such heart-shivering tributes as that to Rose Aylmer: coarse as the bumpkins on the sheep wolds of Lincoln, and yet with as fine subtleties in him as belonged to the young Greeks who clustered about the writer of the *Œdipus Tyrannus.*

The " *First Gentleman.*"

King George IV. was an older man than any of those we have commented on; indeed, he was a prematurely old man at sixty-five — feeling the shivers and the stings of his wild life: I suppose no one ever felt the approaches of age more mortifyingly. He had counted so much on being the fine gentleman to the last — such a height,

such a carriage, such a grace ! It was a dark day
for him when his mirror showed wrinkles that his
cosmetics would not cover, and a stoop in the
shoulders which his tailors could not bolster out of
sight. Indeed, in his later years he shrunk from
exposure of his infirmities, and kept his gouty step
out of reach of the curious, down at Windsor,
where he built a cottage in a wood ; and arranged
his drives through the Park so that those who had
admired this Apollo at his best should never know
of his shakiness. Thither went his conclave of
political advisers — sometimes Canning, the wonderful orator — sometimes the Duke of Wellington,
with the honors of Waterloo upon him — sometimes
young Sir Robert Peel, just beginning to make his
influence felt ; oftener yet, Charles Greville, whose
memoirs are full of piquant details about the royal
household — not forgetting that army of tailors
and hair-dressers who did their best to assuage
the misery and gratify the vanities of the gouty
king. And when he died — which he hated exceedingly to do — in 1830, there came to light
such a multitude of waistcoats, breeches, canes,
snuff-boxes, knee-buckles, whips, and wigs, as I

suppose were never heaped before around any
man's remains. The first gentleman in Europe
could not, after all, carry these things with him.
His brother, William IV., who succeeded him, was
a bluff old Admiral — with not so high a sense of
the proprieties of life as George; but honester
even in his badnesses (which were very many) and,
with all his coarseness and vulgarity, carrying a
brusque, sailor-like frankness that half redeemed
his peccadilloes. In those stormy times which belonged to the passage of the Reform Bill of 1832,
he showed nerve and pluck, and if he split the air
pretty often with his oaths, he never offended by
a wearying dilettanteism, or by foppery. In the
year 1837 he died; and then and there began —
within the memory of a good many of us old
stagers — that reign of his young niece Victoria,
daughter of his brother, the Duke of Kent (who
had died seventeen years before)—which reign
still continues, and is still resplendent with the
virtues of the Sovereign and the well-being of
her people.

Under these several royal hands, the traditional
helpfulness to men of letters had declared itself in

pensions and civil appointments; Southey had
come to his laureateship, and his additional pension; we found the venerable Wordsworth making
a London pilgrimage for a "kissing of hands,"
and the honor of a royal stipend; Walter Scott
had received his baronetcy at the hands of George
IV., and that dilettante sovereign would have
taken Byron (whom we shall presently encounter)
patronizingly by the hand, except the fiery poet —
scenting slights everywhere — had flamed up in
that spirit of proud defiance, which afterward declared itself with a fury of denunciation in the
Irish Avatar (1821).

Hazlitt and Hallam.

Another noticeable author of this period, whose
cynicism kept him very much by himself, was
William Hazlitt; * he was the son of a clergyman

---

* William Hazlitt, b. 1778; d. 1830. *Characters of Shakespeare,* 1817 ; *Table Talk,* 1821; *Liber Amoris,* 1823; *Life
of Napoleon,* 1828; *Life* (by Grandson), 1867; a later book
of memoirs, *Four Generations of a Literary Family,* appeared 1897. (It gave nothing essentially new, and was
quickly withdrawn from sale.)

and very precocious — hearing Coleridge preach
in his father's pulpit at Wem in Shropshire, and
feeling his ambition stirred by the notice of that
poet, who was attracted by the shrewd speech and
great forehead of the boy. Young Hazlitt drifts
away from such early influences to Paris and
to painting—he thinking to master that art. But
in this he does nothing satisfying ; he next appears in London, to carve a way to fame with his
pen. He is an acute observer ; he is proud ; he
is awkward ; he is shy. Charles Lamb and sister
greatly befriend him and take to him ; and he,
with his hate of conventionalisms, loves those
Lamb chambers and the whist parties, where he
can go, in whatever slouch costume he may choose ;
poor Mary Lamb, too, perceiving that he has
a husband-ish hankering after a certain female
friend of hers — blows hot and cold upon it, in
her quaint little notelets, with a delighted and an
undisguised sense of being a party to their little
game. It ended in a marriage at last ; not without its domestic infelicities ; but these would be
too long, and too dreary for the telling. Mr.
Hazlitt wrote upon a vast variety of topics — upon

art, and the drama, upon economic questions,
upon politics — as wide in his range as Leigh
Hunt; and though he was far more trenchant,
more shrewd, more disputatious, more thoughtful,
he did lack Hunt's easy pliancy and grace of touch.
Though a wide reader and acute observer, Hazlitt does not contend or criticise by conventional
rules; his law of measurement is not by old syn-
tactic, grammatic, or dialectic practices; there's
no imposing display of critical implements (by
which some operators dazzle us), but he cuts —
quick and sharp — to the point at issue. We
never forget his strenuous, high-colored personality, and the seething of his prejudices — whether
his talk is of Napoleon (in which he is not reverent of average British opinion), or of Sir Joshua
Reynolds, or of Burke's brilliant oratorical apos-
trophes. But with fullest recognition of his acuteness, and independence, there remains a disposition (bred by his obstinacies and shortcomings)
to take his conclusions *cum grano salis*. He never
quite disabuses our mind of the belief that he is a
paid advocate; he never conquers by calm; and,
upon the whole, impresses one as a man who

found little worth the living for in this world, and counted upon very little in any other.

The historian, Henry Hallam,* on the other hand, who was another notable literary character of this epoch, was full of all serenities of character — even under the weight of such private griefs as were appalling. He was studious, honest, staid — with a great respect for decorum; he would have gravitated socially — as he did — rather to Holland House than to the chambers where Lamb presided over the punch-bowl. In describing the man one describes his histories; slow, calm, steady even to prosiness, yet full; not entertaining in a gossipy sense; not brilliant; scarce ever eloquent. If he is in doubt upon a point he tells you so; if there has been limitation to his research, there is no concealment of it; I think, upon the whole, the honestest of all English historians. In his search for truth, neither party, nor tradition, nor religious scruples make him waver. None can make their historic journey through the Middle Ages

---

* Henry Hallam, b. 1777; d. 1859. *Middle Ages,* 1818. *Literature of Europe,* 1837–39. Sketch of *Life,* by Dean Milman in *Transactions of Royal Society,* vol. x.

without taking into account the authorities he has brought to notice, and the path that he has scored.

And yet there is no atmosphere along that path as he traces it. People and towns and towers and monarchs pile along it, clearly defined, but in dead shapes. He had not the art — perhaps he would have disdained the art — to touch all these with picturesque color, and to make that page of the world's history glow and palpitate with life.

Among those great griefs which weighed upon the historian, and to which allusion has been made, I name that one only with which you are perhaps familiar — I mean the sudden death of his son Arthur, a youth of rare accomplishments — counted by many of more brilliant promise than any young Englishman of his time — yet snatched from life, upon a day of summer's travel, as by a thunderbolt. He lies buried in Clevedon Church, which overhangs the waters of Bristol Channel; and his monument is Tennyson's wonderful memorial poem.

I will not quote from it; but cite only the lines "out of which" (says Dr. John Brown), "as out of the well of the living waters of Love, flows forth all *In Memoriam.*"

> " Break—break—break
>   At the foot of thy crags, O sea :
>   But the tender grace of a day that is dead
>   Will never come back to me.
> And the stately ships go on
>   To their haven under the hill ;
>   But O, for the touch of a vanished hand
>   And the sound of a voice that is still."

I have purposely set before you two strongly contrasted types of English literary life in that day — in William Hazlitt and Henry Hallam — the first representing very nearly what we would call the Bohemian element — ready to-day for an article in the *Edinburgh Review,* and to-morrow for a gibe in the *Examiner,* or a piece of diablerie in the *London Magazine ;* Hallam, on the other hand, representing the sober and orderly traditions, colored by the life and work of such men as Hume, Roscoe, and Gibbon.

Queen of a Salon.

Another group of literary people, of a very varied sort, we should have found in the salons

of my Lady Blessington,* who used to hold court
on the Thames — now by Piccadilly, and again at
Gore House — in the early part of this century.
She was herself a writer ; nor is her personal history without its significance, as an outgrowth of
times when George IV. was setting the pace for
those ambitions of social distinction.

She was the quick-witted daughter of an Irish
country gentleman of the Lucius O'Trigger sort —
nicknamed Beau Power. He loved a whip and
fast horses — also dogs, powder, and blare. He
wore white-topped boots, with showy frills and
ruffles ; he drank hard, swore harder — wasted his
fortune, abused his wife, but was "very fine" to
the end. He was as cruel as he was fine ; shot a
peasant once, in cold blood, and dragged him home
after his saddle beast. He worried his daughter, Marguerite (Lady Blessington), into marrying, at fifteen, a man whom she detested. It

---

* Marguerite Power (Countess of Blessington), b. 1789;
d. 1849; m. Captain Farmer, 1804; m. Earl of Blessington,
1817. 1822-1829, travelling on Continent. *Idler in Italy*,
1839-40 (first novel, about 1833). *Conversations with Lord
Byron*, 1834. Her special *reign* in London, 1831 to 1848.

gave relief, however, from paternal protection,
until the husband proved worse than the father,
and separation ensued — made good (after some
years of tumultuous, uneasy life) by the violent
and providential death of the recreant husband.
Shortly after, she married Lord Blessington, a rich
Irish nobleman, very much blasé, seven years
her senior, but kind and always generous with
her. Then came travel in a princely way over the
Continent, with long stays in pleasant places, and
such lavish spendings as put palaces at their dis-
posal — of all which a readable and gossipy record
is given in her *Idler in Italy* and *Idler in France*
— books well known, in their day, in America.
Of course she encountered in these ramblings
Landor, Shelley, Byron, and all notable Englishmen, and when she returned to London it was to
establish that brilliant little court already spoken
of. She was admirably fitted for sovereign of
such a court; she was witty, ready, well-
instructed; was beautiful, too, and knew every
art of the toilet.*

---

* There is a very interesting, but by no means flattered,
account of Lady Blessington and of her dinners and recep-

More than this, she was mistress of all the pretty and delicate arts of conciliation; had amazing aptitude for accommodating herself to different visitors — flattering men without letting them know they were flattered — softening difficulties, bringing enemies together, magnetizing the most obstinate and uncivil into acquiescence with her rules of procedure. Withal she had in large development those Irish traits of generosity and cheer, with a natural, winning way, which she studied to make more and more taking. One of those women who, with wit, prettiness, and grace, count it the largest, as it is (to them) the most agreeable duty of life, to be forever making social conquests, and forever reaping the applause of drawing-rooms. And if we add to the smiles and the witty banter and the persuasive tones of our lady, the silken hangings, the velvet carpets, the mirrors multiplying inviting alcoves, with paintings by Cattermole or Stothard, and marbles, maybe by Chantrey or Westmacott, and music in its set time by the best of London masters, and

---

tions in Greville's *Journal of the Reign of Queen Victoria*, chapter iv., p. 167, vol. i.

cooking in its season as fine as the music, — and we shall be at no loss to measure the attractions of Gore House, and to judge of the literary and social aspects which blazed there on the foggy banks of the Thames. No wonder that old Samuel Rogers, prince of epicures, should love to carry his pinched face and his shrunk shanks into such sunny latitudes. Moore, too, taking his mincing steps into those regions, would find banquets to remind him of the Bowers of Bendemeer. Possibly, too, the Rev. Sydney Smith, without the fear of Lady Holland in his heart or eyes, may have pocketed his dignity as Canon of St. Paul's and gone thither to taste the delights of the table or of the talk. Even Hallam, or Southey (on his rare visits to town), may have gone there. Lady Blessington was always keenly awake for such arrivals. Even Brougham used to take sometimes his clumsy presence to her brilliant home ; and so, on occasion, did that younger politician, and accomplished gentleman, Sir Robert Peel. Procter — better known as Barry Cornwall — the song-writer, was sure to know his way to those doors and to be welcomed ; and Leigh

IV.—12

Hunt was always eager to play off his fine speeches amid such surroundings of wine and music.

The Comte d'Orsay, artist and man of letters, who married (1827) a daughter of Lord Blessington (step-daughter of the Countess), was a standing ornament of the house; and rivalling him in their cravats and other millinery were two young men who had long careers before them. These were Benjamin Disraeli and Edward Lytton Bulwer.

Young Bulwer and Disraeli.

It was some years before the passage of the Reform bill, and before the death of George IV., that Bulwer * blazed out in *Pelham* (1828), *The Disowned*, and *Devereux*, making conquest of the novel-reading town, at a time when *Quentin Durward* (1823) was not an old book, and *Woodstock*

---

* Edward L. Bulwer (Lord Lytton), b. 1803; d. 1873; *Pelham*, 1828; *Rienzi*, 1835; *Caxton Novels*, 1849–53; *Richelieu*, 1839; his *Biography* (never fully completed) has been written by his son, the second Lord Lytton. It is doubtful, however, if its developments, and inevitable counter-developments, have brought any access of honor to the elder Bulwer.

(1826) still fresh. And if Pelhamism had its speedy subsidence, the same writer put such captivating historic garniture and literary graces about the Italian studies of *Rienzi*, and of the *Last Days of Pompeii*, as carry them now into most libraries, and insure an interested reading — notwithstanding a strong sensuous taint and sentimental extravagances.

He had scholarship; he had indefatigable industry; he had abounding literary ambitions and enthusiasms, but he had no humor; I am afraid he had not a very sensitive conscience; and he had no such pervading refinement of literary taste as to make his work serve as the exemplar for other and honester workers.

Benjamin Disraeli * in those days overmatched him in cravats and in waistcoats, and was the veriest fop of all fop-land. No more beautiful accessory could be imagined to the drawing-room receptions over which Lady Blessington presided,

---

* Benjamin Disraeli (Lord Beaconsfield), b. 1804; d. 1881. *Vivian Grey*, 1826-27; *Contarini Fleming*, 1832; *Coningsby*, 1844; *Lothair*, 1870. Was Premier, 1867, 1874-80. Created Earl of Beaconsfield, 1876.

and of which the ineffable Comte d'Orsay was a
shining and a fixed light, than this young Hebraic
scion of a great Judean house — whose curls were
of the color of a raven's wing, and whose satin
trumpery was ravishing !

And yet — this young foppish Disraeli, within
fifty years, held the destinies of Great Britain in
his hand, and had endowed the Queen with the
grandest title she had ever worn — that of Empress
of India. Still further, in virtue of his old
friendship for his fellow fop Bulwer, he sends the
son of that novelist (in the person of the second
Lord Lytton) to preside over a nation number-
ing two hundred millions of souls. Whoever can
accomplish these ends with such a people as that
of Great Britain must needs have something in
him beyond mere fitness for the pretty salons of
my Lady Blessington.

And what was it ? Whatever you may count it,
there is surely warrant for telling you something
of his history and his antecedents : Three or
more centuries ago — at the very least — a certain
Jew of Cordova, in Spain, driven out by the
terrors of the Inquisition, went to Venice — estab-

lished himself there in merchandise, and his family
throve there for two hundred years. A century
and a half ago, — when the fortunes of Venice
were plainly on the wane — the head of this Jew-
ish family — Benjamin Disraeli (grandfather of
the one of whom we speak) migrated to England.
This first English Benjamin met with success on
the Exchange of London, and owing to the influences of his wife (who hated all Jewry) he discarded his religious connection with Hebraism, went to
the town of Enfield, a little north of London —
with a good fortune, and lived there the life of a
retired country gentleman. He had a son Isaac,
who devoted himself to the study of literature,
and showed early strong bookish proclivities —
very much to the grief of his father, who had a
shrewd contempt for all such follies. Yet the
son Isaac persisted, and did little else through a
long life, save to prosecute inquiries about the
struggles of authors and the lives of authors
and the work of authors — all ending in that
agglomeration which we know as the *Curiosities
of Literature* — a book which sixty years since
used to be reckoned a necessary part of all well-

equipped libraries; but which — to tell truth —
has very little value; being without any method,
without fulness, and without much accuracy. It
is very rare that so poor a book gets so good a
name, and wears it so long.

Oddly enough, this father, who had devoted a
life to the mere gossip of literature, as it were,
warns his son Benjamin against literary pursuits
(he wrote three or four novels indeed, * but they
are never heard of), and the son studied mostly
under private tutors; there is no full or trust-
worthy private biography of him: but we know
that in the years 1826-1827 — only a short time
before the Lady Blessington coterie was in its best
feather — he wrote a novel called *Vivian Grey*, —
the author being then under twenty-two — which
for a time divided attention with *Pelham*. In club
circles it made even more talk. It is full of pictures of people of the day; Brougham and Wilson Croker, and Southey, and George Canning,
and Mrs. Coutts and Lady Melbourne (Caroline
Lamb), all figure in it. He never gave over, in-

---

* *Vaurien*, 1797; *Flim-Flams*, 1805; *Despotism*, or *Fall
of the Jesuits*, 1811.

deed, putting portraits in his books — as Goldwin Smith can tell us. The larger Reviews were coy of praise and coy of condemnation : indeed 'twas hard to say which way it pointed — socially or politically ; but, for the scandal-mongers, there was in it very appetizing meat. He became a lion of the salons ; and he enjoyed the lionhood vastly. Chalon * painted him in that day — a very Adonis — gorgeous in velvet coat and in ruffled shirt.

But he grew tired of England and made his trip of travel ; it followed by nearly a score of years after that of Childe Harold, and was doubtless largely stimulated by it ; three years he was gone — wandering over all the East, as well as Europe. He came back with an epic (published 1834), believing that it was to fill men's minds, and to conquer a place for him among the great poets of the century. In this he was dismally mistaken ; so he broke his lyre, and that was virtually the last of his poesy. There came, however, out of these journeyings, besides the poem, the stories of *Con-*

---

* A. E. Chalon, an artist much in vogue in the days of "Tokens," — who also painted Lady Blessington,—but of no lasting reputation.

turini Fleming, of *The Young Duke*, and *The Wondrous Tale of Alroy*. These kept his fame alive, but seemed after all only the work of a man playing with literature, rather than of one in earnest.

With ambition well sharpened now, by what he counted neglect, he turned to politics ; as the son of a country gentleman of easy fortune, it was not difficult to make place for himself. Yet, with all the traditions of a country gentleman about him, in his first moves he was not inclined to Tory-ism ; indeed, he startled friends by his radicalism — was inclined to shake hands at the outset with the arch-agitator O'Connell ; but not identi-fying himself closely with either party ; and so, to the last it happened that his sympathies were halved in most extraordinary way ; he had the concurrence of the most staid, Toryish, and conser-vative of country voters ; and no man could, like himself, bring all the jingoes of England howling at his back. Indeed, nothing is more remarkable in his career than his shrewd adaptation of policy to meet existing, or approaching tides of feeling ; he does not avow great convictions of duty, and

stand by them ; but he toys with convictions ;
studies the weakness, as he does the power, of
those with him or against him ; shifts his ground
accordingly ; rarely lacking poise, and the attitude of seeming steadfastness ; whipping with his
scourge of a tongue the little lapses of his adver-
saries till they shrill all over the kingdom ; and
putting his own triumphs — great or small — into
such scenic combination, with such beat of drum,
and blare of trumpet, as to make all England
break out into bravos.* There was not that literary quality in his books, either early or late,
which will give to them, I think, a very long life ;
but there was in the man a quality of shrewdness
and of power which will be long remembered —
perhaps not always to his honor.

I do not yield to any in admiration for the noble
and philanthropic qualities which belong to the
venerable, retired statesman of Hawarden ; yet I

---

* In illustration of his comparatively humble position early,
Greville in his later *Journal*, Chapter XXIV., speaks of
Disraeli's once proposing to Moxon, the publisher, to take
him (Disraeli) into partnership ; Greville says Moxon told him
this.

cannot help thinking that if such a firm and audacious executive hand as belonged to Lord Beaconsfield, had — in the season of General Gordon's
stress at Khartoum — controlled the fleets and
armies of Great Britain, there would have been
quite other outcome to the sad imbroglio in the
Soudan.   When war is afoot, the apostles of peace
are the poorest of directors.

I go back for a moment to that Blessington
Salon — in order to close her story.   There was
a narrowed income — a failure of her jointure
— a shortening of her book sales; but, notwithstanding, there was a long struggle to keep
that brilliant little court alive.   One grows to
like so much the music and the fêtes and the
glitter of the chandeliers, and the unction of
flattering voices !   But at last the ruin came; on
a sudden the sheriffs were there ; and clerks with
their inventories in place of the "Tokens" and
"annuals" — with their gorgeous engravings by
Finden & Heath — which the Mistress had ex-
ploited ; and she hurried off — after the elegant
D'Orsay — to Paris, hoping to rehabilitate herself,
on the Champs Elysées, under the wing of Louis

Napoleon, just elected President. I chanced to see
her in her coupé there, on a bright afternoon early
in 1849 — with elegant silken wraps about her
and a shimmer of the old kindly smile upon her
shrunken face — dashing out to the Bois; but
within three months there was another sharp
change ; she — dead, and her pretty *decolleté* court
at an end forever.

The Poet of Newstead.

The reminiscences and conversations of Lord
Byron, which we have at the hands of Lady
Blessington, belong to a time, of course, much
earlier than her series of London triumphs, and
date with her journeys in Italy. A score of years
at least before ever the chandeliers of her Irish
ladyship were lighted in Gore House, Byron * had

---

* George Noel Gordon (Lord Byron), b. (London) 1788;
d. (Greece) 1824. *Hours of Idleness*, 1807 ; *English Bards*,
etc., 1809 ; *Childe Harold* (2 cantos), 1812 ; *Don Juan*, 1819-
24; Moore's *Life*, 1830 ; Trelawney, *Recollections, etc.*, 1858.
The first volume (Macmillan, 1897) has appeared of a new
edition of Byron's works, with voluminous notes (in over-fine
print) by William Ernest Henley. The editorial stand-point
may be judged by this averment from the preface, — "the sole

gone sailing away from England under a storm of wrath ; and he never came back again. Indeed it is not a little extraordinary that one of the most typical of English poets, should—like Landor, with whom he had many traits in common—have passed so little of his active life on English ground. Like Landor, he loved England most when England was most behind him. Like Landor, he was gifted with such rare powers as belonged to few Englishmen of that generation. In Landor these powers, so far as they expressed themselves in literary form, were kept in check by the iron rulings of a scrupulous and exacting craftsmanship ; while in Byron they broke all trammels, whether of craftsmanship or reason, and glowed and blazed the more by reason of their audacities. Both were prone to great tempests of wrath which gave to both furious joys, and, I think, as furious regrets.

English poet bred since Milton to live a master-influence in the world at large."

Another full edition of works, with editing by Earl of Lovelace (grandson of Byron), is announced as shortly to appear from the press of Murray in London, and of Scribners in New York.

Byron came by his wrathfulness in good hereditary fashion — as we shall find if we look back only a little way into the records of that Newstead family. Newstead Abbey (more properly Priory, the archæologists tell us) is the name of that great English home — half a ruin — associated with the early years of the poet, but never for much time or in any true sense a home of his own. It is some ten miles north of Nottingham, in an interesting country, where lay the old Sherwood Forest, with its traditions of Robin Hood ; there is a lichened Gothic front which explains the Abbey name ; there are great rambling corridors and halls ; there is a velvety lawn, with the monument to "Boatswain," the poet's dog ; but one who goes there — with however much of Byronic reading in his or her mind — will not, I think, warm toward the locality ; and the curious foot-traveller will incline to trudge away in a hunt for Annesley, and the "Antique Oratory."

Well, in that ancient home, toward the end of the last century, there lived, very much by himself, an old Lord Byron, who some thirty years before, in a fit of wild rage, had killed a neighbor and kinsman of the name of Chaworth; there was indeed a little show of a duel about the murder — which was done in a London tavern, and by candle-light. His peerage, however, only saved this "wicked lord," as he was called, from prison; and at Newstead his life smouldered out in 1798, under clouds of hate, and of distrust. His son was dead before him; so was his grandson, the last heir in direct line; but he had a younger brother, John, who was a great seaman—who published accounts of his voyages,* which seem always to have been stormy, and which lend, maybe, some realistic touches to the shipwreck scenes in "Don Juan." A son of this voyager was the father of the poet, and was reputed to be as full of wrath and turbulence as his uncle who killed the Chaworth; and his life was as thick with disaster as that of the unlucky voyager. His first marriage was a runaway one with a titled lady, whose heart he broke, and who died leaving that lone daughter who became the most worthy Lady Augusta

---

* Byron's *Narrative,* published in the first volume of *Hawkesworth's Collection.* Hon. John Byron, Admiral, etc., was at one time Governor of Newfoundland; b. 1723; d. 1786.

Leigh. For second wife he married Miss Gordon, a Scotch heiress, the mother of the poet, whose fortune he squandered, and whose heart also he would have broken — if it had been of a breaking quality. With such foregoers of his own name, one might look for bad blood in the boy ; nor was his mother saint-like; she had her storms of wrath ; and from the beginning, I think, gave her boy only cruel milk to drink.

His extreme boyhood was passed near to Aberdeen, with the Highlands not far off. How much those scenes impressed him, we do not know; but that some trace was left may be found in verses written near his death :—

> " He who first met the Highland's swelling blue
>   Will love each peak that shows a kindred hue ;
>   Hail in each crag a friend's familiar face
>   And clasp the mountain in his mind's embrace."

When the boy was ten, the wicked lord who had killed the Chaworth died ; and the Newstead inheritance fell to the young poet. We can imagine with what touch of the pride that shivers through so many of his poems, this lad — just lame enough to make him curse that unlucky fate — paced first down the hall at Newstead — thenceforth master there — a Peer of England.

But the estate was left in sorry condition; the mother could not hold it as a residence; so they went to Nottingham — whereabout the boy seems to have had his first schooling. Not long afterward we find him at Harrow, not far out of London, where he makes one or two of the few friendships which abide; there, too, he gives first evidence of his power over language.

It is at about this epoch, also, that on his visits to Nottingham — which is not far from the Chaworth home of Annesley — comes about the spinning of those little webs of romance which are twisted afterward into the beautiful Chaworth "Dream." It is an old story to tell, yet how everlastingly fresh it keeps!

> "The maid was on the eve of womanhood;
> The boy had fewer summers, but his heart
> Had far outgrown his years, and to his eye
> There was but one beloved face on earth,
> And that was shining on him; he had looked
> Upon it till it could not pass away;
> He had no breath, nor being, but in hers,

She was his voice . . . upon a tone,
A touch of hers, his blood would ebb and flow,
And his cheek change tempestuously — his heart
Unknowing of its cause of agony."

As a matter of fact, Miss Chaworth was two years older, and far more mature than he; she was gentle too, and possessed of a lady-like calm, which tortured him — since he could not break it down. Indeed, through all the time when he was sighing, she was looking over his head at Mr. Musters — who was bluff and hearty, and who rode to the hounds, and was an excellent type of the rollicking, self-satisfied, and beef-eating English squire — whom she married.

Early Verse and Marriage.

After this episode came Cambridge, and those *Hours of Idleness* which broke out into verse, and caught the scathing lash of Henry Brougham — then a young, but well-known, advocate, who was conspiring with Sydney Smith and Jeffrey (as I have told you) to renovate the world through the pages of the *Edinburgh Review.*

But this lashing brought a stinging reply; and the clever, shrewd, witty couplets of Byron's satire

IV.—13

upon the Scottish Reviewers (1809), convinced all
scholarly readers that a new and very piquant
pen had come to the making of English verse.
Nor were Byron's sentimentalisms of that day all so
crude and ill-shapen as Brougham would have led
the public to suppose. I quote a fragment from
a little poem under date of 1808—he just twenty :

> " The dew of the morning
>   Sunk chill on my brow
> It felt like the warning
>   Of what I feel now,
> Thy vows are all broken
>   And light is thy fame ;
> I hear thy name spoken,
>   And share in its shame.
>
> " They name thee before me,
>   A knell to mine ear ;
> A shudder comes o'er me —
>   Why wert thou so dear?
> They know not I knew thee,
>   Who knew thee too well ;
> Long, long shall I rue thee
>   Too deeply to tell."

Naturally enough, our poet is beaming with the
success of his satire, which is widely read, and
which has made him foes of the first rank ; but
what cares he for this ? He goes down with a

company of fellow roisterers, and makes the old
walls of Newstead ring with the noisy celebration
of his twenty-first birthday; and on the trail of that
country revel, and with the sharp, ringing couplets of his "English Bards" crackling on the public ear, he breaks away for his first joyous experience of Continental travel. This takes him
through Spain and to the Hellespont and among
the isles of Greece — seeing visions there and
dreaming dreams, all which are braided into that
tissue of golden verse we know as the first two
cantos of *Childe Harold.*

On his return, and while as yet this poem of
travel is on the eve of publication, he prepares
himself for a new *coup* in Parliament — being
not without his oratorical ambitions. It was
in February of 1812 that he made his maiden
speech in the House of Lords — carefully word-
ed, calm, not without quiet elegancies of dic-
tion — but not meeting such reception as his
extravagant expectation demanded; whatever he
does, he wishes met with a tempest of approval; a
dignified welcome, to his fiery nature, seems cold.

But the publication of *Childe Harold,* only a

short time later, brings compensating torrents of
praise. His satire had piqued attention without
altogether satisfying it; there was little academic
merit in it — none of the art which made *Absa-
lom and Achitophel* glow, or which gleamed
upon the sword-thrusts of the *Dunciad;* but its
stabs were business-like; its couplets terse, slash-
ing, and full of truculent, scorching *vires iræ.*
This other verse, however, of *Childe Harold* —
which took one upon the dance of waves and under the swoop of towering canvass to the groves of
" Cintra's glorious Eden," and among those Spanish vales where Dark Guadiana "rolls his power
along ; " and thence on, by proud Seville, and
fair Cadiz, to those shores of the Egean, where

> " Still his honeyed wealth Hymettus yields,—" *

---

* The short line is not enough. We must give the burden
of that apostrophe to the land of Hellas, though only in a note :

> " Sweet are thy groves, and verdant are thy fields;
>   Thine olive ripe as when Minerva smiled,
> And still his honeyed wealth Hymettus yields.
>   There the blithe bee his fragrant fortress builds,
> The free-born wanderer of the mountain air;
>   Apollo still thy long, long summer gilds,
> Still in his beams Mendeli's marbles glare,
>   Art, Glory, Freedom fail, but Nature still is fair."

was of quite another order. There is in it, moreover, the haunting personality of the proud, broken-
spirited wanderer, who tells the tale and wraps
himself in the veil of mysterious and piquant sorrows : Withal there is such dash and spirit, such
mastery of language, such marvellous descriptive power, such subtle pauses and breaks, carrying echoes beyond the letter — as laid hold on
men and women — specially on women — in a way
that was new and strange. And this bright me-
teor had flashed athwart a sky where such stars as
Southey, and Scott, and Rogers, and the almost
forgotten Crabbe, and Coleridge, and Wordsworth
had been beaming for many a day. Was it
strange that the doors of London should be flung
wide open to this fresh, brilliant singer who had
blazed such a path through Spain and Greece, and
who wore a coronet upon his forehead ?

He was young, too, and handsome as the morning ; and must be mated — as all the old dowagers
declared. So said his friends — his sister chiefest
among them ; and the good Lady Melbourne
(mother-in-law of Lady Caroline Lamb) — not
without discreet family reasons of her own — fixed

upon her charming niece, Miss Milbanke, as the
one with whom the new poet should be coupled,
to make his way through the wildernesses before
him.   And there were other approvals ; even Tom
Moore — who, of all men, knew his habits best —
saying a reluctant " Yes " — after much hesitation.
And so, through a process of coy propositions and
counter-propositions, the marriage was arranged
at last, and came about down at Seaham House
(near Stockton-on-Tees), the country home of the
father, Sir Ralph Milbanke.

> "Her face was fair, but was not that which made
>   The starlight of his boyhood; as he stood
> Even at the altar, o'er his brow there came
>   The self-same aspect, and the quivering shock
> That in the Antique Oratory shook
>   His bosom in its solitude; and then —
> As in that hour — a moment o'er his face
>   The tablet of unutterable thoughts
> Was traced; and then it faded as it came,
>   And he stood calm and quiet, and he spoke
> The fitting vows, but heard not his own words,
>   And all things reeled around him." *

---

* I cite that part of the "Dream" which, though written
much time after, was declared by the poet, and by both
friends and foes, to represent faithfully his attitude — both
moral and physical — on the occasion of his marriage.

Yet the service went on to its conclusion ; and
the music pealed, and the welcoming shouts broke
upon the air, and the adieux were spoken ; and
together, they two drove away — into the darkness.

CHAPTER VI.

OUR last chapter brought us into the presence of that vivacious specimen of royalty, George IV., who "shuffled off this mortal coil" in the year 1830, and was succeeded by that rough-edged, seafaring brother of his, William IV. This admiral-king was not brilliant; but we found brilliancy — of a sort — in the acute and disputatious essayist, William Hazlitt; yet he was far less companionable than acute, and contrasted most unfavorably with that serene and most worthy gentleman, Hallam, the historian. We next encountered the accomplished and showy Lady Blessington — the type of many a one who throve in those days, and who had caught somewhat of the glitter that radiated from the royal trappings of George the Fourth. We saw Bulwer, among others, in her salon ; and we lingered longer over the wonderful career of that Disraeli, who died as Lord Beaconsfield — the most widely known man in Great Britain.

We then passed to a consideration of that other wonderful adventurer — yet the inheritor of an English peerage — who had made his futile beginning in politics, and a larger beginning in poetry. To his career, which was left half-finished, we now recur.

Lord Byron a Husband.

As we left him — you will remember — there was a jangle of marriage-bells ; and a wearisome jangle it proved. Indeed Byron's marriage-bells were so preposterously out of tune, and lent their discord in such disturbing manner to the whole current of his life, that it may be worth our while to examine briefly the conditions under which the discord began. It is certain that all the gossips of London had been making prey of this match of the poetic hero of the hour for much time before its consummation.

Was he seeking a fortune ? Not the least in the world ; for though the burden of debt upon

his estates was pressing him sorely, and his extravagances were reckless, yet large sums accruing
from his swift-written tales of the "Corsair,"
"Lara," and "Bride of Abydos" were left un-
touched, or lavishly bestowed upon old or new
friends ; his liberality in those days was most ex-
ceptional ; nor does it appear that he had any
very definite notion of the pecuniary aid which
his bride might bring to him.   She had, indeed, in
her own right, what was a small sum measured
by their standards of living; and her expect-
ancies, that might have justified the title of heiress
(which he sometimes gives to her in his journal),
were then quite remote.

As for social position, there could be by such
marriage no gain to him, for whom already the
doors of England were flung wide open.   Did he
seek the reposeful dignity of a home ?   There may
have been such fancies drifting by starts through
his mind ; but what crude fancies they must have
been with a man who had scarcely lived at peace
with his own mother, and whose only notion of
enjoyment in the house of his ancestors was in the
transport to Newstead of a roistering company of

boon companions — followed by such boisterous
revels there, and such unearthly din and ghostly
frolics, as astounded the neighborhood !

The truth is, he marched into that noose of
matrimony as he would have ordered a new
suit from his tailor. When this whim had first
seized him, he had written off formal proposals to
Miss Milbanke — whom he knew at that time only
slightly ; and she, with very proper prudence, was
non-committal in her reply — though suggesting
friendly correspondence. In his journal of a little later date we have this entry :

"November 30, 1813 [some fourteen months before the
marriage]. Yesterday a very pretty letter from Annabella
[the full name was Anna Isabella], which I answered. What
an odd situation and friendship is ours ! Without one spark
of love on either side. She is a very superior woman, and
very little spoiled . . . a girl of twenty, an only child
and a *savante*, who has always had her own way."

This evidently does not promise a very ardent
correspondence. Nay, it is quite possible that the
quiet reserve he encounters here, does offer a re-
freshing contrast to the heated gush of which he
is the subject in that Babel of London ; maybe,

too, there is something in the reserve and the as-
sured dignity which reminds him of that earlier
idol of his worship — Miss Chaworth of Annesley.

However, three months after this last allusion
to Miss Milbanke, we have another entry in his
journal, running thus :

"January 16, 1814. A wife would be my salvation. I am
getting rather into an admiration for C——, youngest
sister of F——. [This is not Miss Milbanke — observe.]
That she won't love me is very probable, nor shall I love
her. The business would probably be arranged between the
papa and me."

Perhaps it was in allusion to this new caprice
that he writes to Moore, a few months later :

"Had Lady —— appeared to wish it, or even not to op-
pose it, I would have gone on, and very possibly married,
with the same indifference which has frozen over the Black
Sea of almost all my passions. . . . Obstacles the
slightest even, stop me." (*Moore's Byron*, p. 255.)

And it is in face of some such obstacle, lifting
suddenly, that he flashes up, and over, into new
proposals to Miss Milbanke; these are quietly accepted — very likely to his wonderment; for he
says, in a quick ensuing letter to Moore :

"I certainly did not dream that she was attached to me, which it seems she has been for some time. I also thought her of a very cold disposition, in which I was also mistaken; it is a long story, and I won't trouble you with it. As to her virtues, and so on, you will hear enough of them (for she is a kind of *pattern* in the north) without my running into a display on the subject."

A little over two months after the date of this they were married, and he writes to Murray in the same week :

"The marriage took place on the 2d inst., so pray make haste and congratulate away." [And to Moore, a few days later.] "I was married this day week. The parson has pronounced it; Perry has announced it, and the *Morning Post*, also, under head of 'Lord Byron's marriage'— as if it were a fabrication and the puff direct of a new stay-maker."

A month and a half later, in another Moore letter, alluding to the death of the Duke of Dorset (an old friend of his), he says :

"There was a time in my life when this event would have broken my heart; and all I can say for it now is — that it isn't worth breaking."

Two more citations, and I shall have done with this extraordinary record. In March, 1815 (the marriage having occurred in January), he writes

to Moore from the house of his father-in-law, Sir
Ralph Milbanke — a little northward of the Tees,
in County Durham :

> "I am in such a state of sameness and stagnation, and so
> totally occupied in consuming the fruits, and sauntering, and
> playing dull games at cards, and yawning, and trying to read
> old *Annual Registers* and the daily papers, and gathering
> shells on the shore, and watching the growth of stunted goose-
> berries in the garden, that I have neither time nor sense to
> say more than yours ever — B."

A Stay in London.

On leaving the country for a new residence in
London, his growing cheer and spirits are very
manifest :

> "I have been very comfortable here. Bell is in health, and
> unvaried good humor. But we are all in the agonies of
> packing. . . . I suppose by this hour to-morrow I shall
> be stuck in the chariot with my chin upon a band-box. I
> have prepared, however, another carriage for the abigail, and
> all the trumpery which our wives drag along with them."

Well, there follows a year or more of this
coupled life — with what clashings we can imagine.
Old Ralph Milbanke is not there to drawl through
his after-dinner stories, and to intrude his re-

straining presence. The poet finds things to watch about the clubs and the theatres — quite other than the stunted gooseberries that grew in his father-in-law's garden. Nothing is more sure than that the wilful audacities, and selfishness, and temper of the poet, put my lady's repose and dignities and perfection to an awful strain. Nor is it to be wondered at, if the mad and wild indiscretions of the husband should have provoked some quiet and galling counter indiscretions on the part of her ladyship.

It is alleged, for instance, that on an early occasion — and at the suggestion of a lady companion of the august mistress — there was an inspection of my lord's private papers, and a sending home to their writers of certain highly perfumed notelets found therein ; and we can readily believe that when this instance of wifely zeal came to his lordship's knowledge he broke into a strain of remark which was *not* precisely that of the " Hebrew Melodies." Doubtless he carries away from such encounter a great reserve of bottled wrath — not so much against her ladyship personally, as against the stolid proprieties, the un-

bending scruples, the ladylike austerities, and the
cool, elegant dowager-dignities she represents.
Fancy a man who has put such soul as he has,
and such strength and hope and pride as he has,
into those swift poems, which have taken his
heart's blood to their making — fancy him, asked
by the woman who has set out to widen his hopes
and life by all the helps of wifehood, *"When —
pray — he means to give up those versifying habits
of his?"* No, I do not believe he resented this in
language. I don't believe he argued the point; I
don't believe he made defence of versifying habits;
but I imagine that he regarded her with a dazed
look, and an eye that saw more than it seemed to
see — an eye that discerned broad shallows in her,
where he had hoped for pellucid depths. I think
he felt then — if never before — a premonition
that their roads would not lie long together. And
yet it gave him a shock — not altogether a pleasant one, we may be sure — when Sir Ralph, the
father-in-law, to whose house she had gone on a
visit, wrote him politely to the effect that — "she
would never come back." Such things cannot be
pleasant; at least, I should judge not.

And so, she thinks something more of marriage than as some highly reckoned conventionality — under whose cover bickerings may go on and spend their force, and the decent twin masks be always worn. And in him, we can imagine lingering traces of a love for the feminine features in her — for the grace, the dignity, the sweet face, the modesties — but all closed over and buckled up, and stanched by the everlasting and all encompassing buckram that laces her in, and that has so little of the compensating instinctive softness and yieldingness which might hold him in leash and win him back. The woman who cannot — on occasions — put a weakness into her forgiveness, can never put a vital strength into her persuasion.

But they part, and part forever; the only wonder is they had not parted before; and still another wonder is, that there should have been zealous hunt for outside causes when so many are staringly apparent within the walls of home. I do not believe that Byron would have lived at peace with one woman in a thousand; I do not believe that Lady Byron would have lived at peace with one man in a hundred. The computation is

IV.—14

largely in her favor; although it does not imply necessity for his condemnation as an utter brute. Even as he sails away from England — from which he is hunted with hue and cry, and to whose shores he is never again to return — he drops a farewell to her with such touches of feeling in it, that one wonders — and future readers always will wonder — with what emotions the mother and his child may have read it :

> " Fare thee well and if for ever, *
>   Still for ever — fare thee well!
> Even tho' unforgiving — never
>   'Gainst thee shall my heart rebel.
>
> .   .   .   .   .
>
> Love may sink by slow decay
>   But, by sudden wrench, believe not
> Hearts can thus be torn away.

---

* This poem appeared about the middle of April, 1816. The final break in his relations with Lady Byron had occurred, probably, in early February of the same year. On December 10, 1815, his daughter Ada was born; and on April 25th, next ensuing, he sailed away from England forever. Byron insisted that the poem (" Fare thee well "), though written in sincerity, was published against his inclinations, through the over-zeal of a friend.—*Moore's Life*, p. 526, vol. i.

And when thou would'st solace gather,
When our child's first accents flow,
  Wilt thou teach her to say ' Father '
Though his care she must forego?
  When her little hands shall press thee,
When her lip to thine is prest,
  Think of him whose prayer shall bless thee;
Think of him thy love has blessed.
  Should her lineaments resemble
Those thou never more may'st see,
  Then thy heart will softly tremble
With a pulse yet true to me;
  All my faults perchance thou knowest,
All my madness none can know,
  All my hopes where'er thou goest
Wither — yet, with thee they go.
Every feeling hath been shaken;
  Pride which not a world could bow,
Bows to thee — by thee forsaken,
  Even my soul forsakes me now.
But 'tis done, all words are idle;
  Words from *me* are vainer still;
But the thoughts we cannot bridle
  Force their way, without the will.
Fare thee well! thus disunited,
  Torn from every nearer tie,
Seared in heart and lone, and blighted —
  More than this, I scarce can die."

I should have felt warranted in giving some in-
telligible account of the poet's infelicities at home

were it only to lead up to this exhibit of his wondrous literary skill; but I find still stronger reasons in the fact that the hue and cry which followed upon his separation from his wife seemed to exalt the man to an insolent bravado, and a challenge of all restraint — under which his genius flamed up with new power, and with a blighting splendor.

Exile.

It was on the 25th of April, 1816 (he being then in his twenty-eighth year), that he bade England adieu forever, and among the tenderest of his leave-takings was that from his sister, who had .vainly sought to make smooth the difficulties in his home, and who (until Lady Byron had fallen into the blindness of dotage) retained her utmost respect. I cannot forbear quoting two verses from a poem addressed to this devoted sister :

" Though the rock of my last hope is shivered
And its fragments are sunk in the wave,
Though I feel that my soul is delivered
To pain — it shall *not* be its slave;
There is many a pang to pursue me;
They may crush — but they shall not contemn,
They may torture, but shall not subdue me,
'Tis of *thee* that I think — not of them.

" From the wreck of the past, which hath perished,
   Thus much I at least may recall,
It hath taught me that what I most cherished
   Deserved to be dearest of all;
In the desert a fountain is springing,
   In the wide waste, there still is a tree,
And a bird in the solitude singing
   Which speaks to my spirit of *thee*."

Never was a man pelted away from his native shores with more anathemas ; never one in whose favor so few appealing voices were heard. It was not so much a memory of his satirical thrusts, as a jealousy begotten by his late extraordinary successes, which had alienated nearly the whole literary fraternity. Only Rogers, Moore, and Scott were among the better known ones who had forgiven his petulant verse, and were openly apologetic and friendly ; while such kind wishers as Lady Holland and Lady Jersey were half afraid to make a show of their sympathies. Creditors, too, of that burdened estate of his, had pushed their executions one upon another — in those days when his torments were most galling — into what was yet called with poor significance his home ; only his title of peer, Moore tells us, at one date saved him from prison.

Yet when he lands in Belgium, he travels — true to his old recklessness — like a prince; with body servants and physician, and a lumbering family coach, with its showy trappings. Waterloo was fresh then, and the wreck and the blood, and the glory of it were all scored upon his brain, and shortly afterward by his fiery hand upon the poem we know so well, and which will carry that streaming war pennon in the face of other generations than ours. Then came the Rhine, with its castles and traditions, glittering afresh in the fresh stories that he wove; and after these his settlement for a while upon the borders of Lake Geneva — where, in some one of these talks of ours we found the studious Gibbon, under his acacia-trees, and where Rousseau left his footprints — never to be effaced — at Clarens and Meillerie. One would suppose that literature could do no more with such outlooks on lake and mountain, as seem to mock at language.

And yet the wonderful touch of Byron has kindled new interest in scenes on which the glowing periods of Rousseau had been lavished. Even the guide-books can none of them complete their record of the region without stealing descriptive gems from his verse ; and his story of the *Prisoner of Chillon* will always — for you and for me — lurk in the shadows that lie under those white castle walls, and in the murmur of the waters that ebb and flow — gently as the poem — all round about their foundations. I may mention that at the date of the Swiss visit, and under the influences and active co-operation of Madame de Staël — then a middle-aged and invalid lady residing at her country seat of Coppet, on the borders of Geneva Lake — Byron did make overtures for a reconciliation with his wife. They proved utterly without avail, even if they were not treated with scorn. And it is worthy of special note that while up to this date all mention of Lady Byron by the poet had been respectful, if not relenting and conciliatory — thereafter the vials of his wrath were opened, and his despairing scorn knew no bounds. Thus, in the "Incantation" — thrust into that uncanny work of *Manfred* — with which he was then at labor — he says :

"Though thou seest me not pass by,
Thou shalt feel me with thine eye,

As a thing that, though unseen,
Must be near thee, and hath been ;
And when, in that secret dread,
Thou hast turned around thy head,
Thou shalt marvel I am not
As thy shadow on the spot ;
And the power which thou dost feel
Shall be what thou must conceal."

Shelley and Godwin.

Another episode of Byron's Swiss life was his encounter there, for the first time, with the poet Shelley.* He, too, was under ban, for reasons that I must briefly make known. Like his brother poet, Shelley was born to a prospective inheritance of title and of wealth. His father was a baronet, shrewd and calculating, and living

---

* Percy Bysshe Shelley, b. 1792; d. (by drowning in Gulf of Spezia) 1822. *Queen Mab*, pub. 1821 (but privately printed 1813); *Alastor*, 1816; *Laon and Cythna* (afterward *Revolt of Islam*), 1818; *Adonais*, 1821. *Life*, by Mrs. Shelley, 1845; Hogg's *Life*, 1858; Rossetti's, 1870. Besides which there is biographic material, more or less full, by Forman, Trelawny, McCarthy, Leigh Hunt, Garnett, and Jeaffreson (*Real Shelley*). *Life*, in *English Men of Letters*, by the late John Addington Symonds; and in 1886, Professor Dowden's work.

by the harshest and baldest of old conventionalisms ; this father had given a warm, brooding care
to the estate left him by Sir Bysshe Shelley (the
grandfather of the poet), who had an American
bringing up — if not an American birth — in the
town of Newark,* N. J. The boy poet had the ad-
vantages of a place at Eton † — not altogether a
favorite there, it would seem ; "passionate in his
resistance to an injury, passionate in his love."
He carried thence to Oxford a figure and a
beauty of countenance that were almost effemi-
nate ; and yet he had a capacity for doubts and
negations that was wondrously masculine. His
scholarship was keen, but not tractable ; he takes
a wide range outside the established order of
studies ; he is a great and unstinted admirer of
the French philosophers, and makes such audacious free-thinking challenge to the church digni-
taries of Oxford that he is expelled — like some-

---

* Rossetti, in *Ency. Britannica*, says, " in Christ Church,
Newark " — as to which item (repeated by Dowden) there has
been some American wonderment !

† July, 1804, to July, 1810; *Athenæum*, No. 3,006, June,
1885.

thing venomous. His father, too, gives him the
cold shoulder at this crisis, and he drifts to London. There he contrives interviews with his
sisters, who are in school at Clapham ; and is de-
coyed into a marriage — before he is twenty —
with a somewhat pretty and over-bold daughter
of a coffee-house keeper, who has acted as a go-
between in communications with his sisters. The
prudent, conventional father is now down upon
him with a vengeance.

But the boy has pluck under that handsome
face of his. He sets out, with his wife — after
sundry wanderings — to redeem Ireland ; but they
who are used to blunderbusses, undervalue
Shelley's fine periods, and his fine face. He is
some time in Wales, too (the mountains there
fastening on his thought and cropping out in after
poems) ; he is in Edinboro', in York, in Keswick
— making his obeisance to the great Southey
(but coming to over-hate of him in after years).
Meantime he has children. Sometimes money
comes from the yielding father — sometimes none ;
he is abstemious ; bread and water mostly his
diet ; his home is without order or thrift or in-

vitingness — the lapses of the hoydenish girl-wife stinging him over and over and through and through.

But Shelley has read Godwin's *Political Justice* — one of those many fine schemes for the world's renovation, by tearing out and burning up most of the old furniture, which make their appearance periodically — and in virtue of his admiration of Godwin, Shelley counts him among the demi-gods of the heaven which he has conjured up. In reality Godwin * was an oldish, rather clumsy, but astute and clever dissenting minister, who had left preaching, and had not only written *Political Justice*, but novels — among them one called *Caleb Williams;* by which you will know him better — if you know him at all. This gave him great reputation in its time. There were critics who ranked him with, or above, Scott — even in fiction. This may tempt you to read *Caleb Will-*

---

* William Godwin, b. 1756; d. 1836. *Political Justice*, 1793; *Caleb Williams*, 1794. William Austen (author of *Peter Rugg*), in his *Letters from London*, 1802–3, describes a visit to Godwin at his cottage — Somerston; notices a portrait of " Mary " (Mrs. Shelley) hanging over the mantel.

iams ; * and if you read it — you will not forget it. It pinches the memory like a vice ; much reading of it might, I should think, engender, in one of vivid imagination, such nightmare stories as " *Called Back* " or " *A Dark Day.* "

But Mr. Godwin had a daughter, Mary (whose mother was that Mary Wollstonecraft, promoted now to a place amongst famous women), and our Shelley going to see Godwin, saw also the daughter Mary — many times over; and these two — having misty and mystic visions of a new order of ethics — ran away together.

It must be said, however, to the credit of Shelley (if credit be the word to use), that when this first wife killed herself — as she did some eighteen months afterward † (whether from grief or other

---

* Miss Martineau (p. 304, vol. ii., *Autobiography*) says that Godwin told her he wrote the first half of *Caleb Williams* in three months, and then stopped for six — finishing it in three more. " This pause," she says, " in the middle of a work so intense, seems to me a remarkable incident."

† Separation took place about the middle of June, 1814; she destroyed herself, November 10, 1816. At one time there had been ugly rumors that she was untrue to him ; and there is some reason to believe that Shelley once entertained this belief, but there is no adequate testimony to that end; God-

cause is doubtful) — he married Miss Godwin; and
it was during the summer preceding this second
marriage that Byron (1816) encountered Shelley
on the shores of Lake Leman. Shelley had already written that wild screed of *Queen Mab*
(privately printed, 1813), giving poetic emphasis
to the scepticism of his Oxford days. He had
published that dreamy poem of *Alastor* — himself
its poet hero, as indeed he was in a large sense of
every considerable poem he wrote. I cite a fragment of it, that you may see what waking and
beguiling voice belonged to the young bard, who
posed there on the Geneva lake beside the more
masculine Byron. He has taken us into forest
depths :

> " One vast mass
> Of mingling shade, whose brown magnificence
> A narrow vale embosoms.
> The pyramids
> Of the tall cedar, overarching, frame
> Most solemn domes within; and far below,
> Like clouds suspended in an emerald sky,
> The ash and the acacia floating, hang

---

win's *dixit* should not count for very much. Dowden leaves
the matter in doubt.

Tremulous and pale.   Like restless serpents clothed
In rainbow and in fire, the parasites
Starred with ten thousand blossoms flowed around
The gray trunks; and as gamesome infants' eyes,
With gentle meanings and most innocent wiles
Fold their beams round the hearts of those that love,
These twine their tendrils with the wedded boughs.
.   .   .   . the woven leaves
Make net-work of the dark blue lights of day
And the night's noontide clearness, mutable
As shapes in the weird clouds.
            One darkest glen
Sends from its woods of musk-rose twined with jasmine
A soul-dissolving odor, to invite
To some more lovely mystery.   Through the dell
Silence and twilight here, twin sisters, keep
Their noonday watch, and sail among the shades
Like vaporous shapes half seen."

And such mysteries and vaporous shapes run
through all his poetic world. He wanders, with
that rarely fine gift of rhythmic speech, as wide
away from the compact sordid world — upon
which Byron always sets foot with a ringing tread
— as ever Spenser in his chase of rainbow crea-
tions.   Yet there were penetrative sinuous influences about that young poet — defiant of law and
wrapt in his pursuit of mysteries — which may
well have given foreign touches of color to Byron's

Manfred or to his *Prometheus.* At any rate, these two souls lay quietly for a time, warped together — like two vessels windbound under mountain shelter.

Byron in Italy.

Byron next goes southward, to riotous life in Venice; where — whether in tradesmen's houses or in palaces upon the Grand Canal, or in country villas upon the Euganean hills — he defies priests and traditions, and order, and law, and decency.

To this period belongs, probably, the conception, if not the execution, of many of those dramas * — as non-playable as ever those of Tennyson — unequal, too, but with passages scattered here and there of great beauty ; masterly aggregation of words smoking with passion, and full of such bullet-like force of expression as only he could command ; but there is no adequate blending of parts to make either stately or well-harmonized march of events toward large and definite issues.

---

* I am reminded that Macready's impersonation of *Werner* was a noted and successful one. *Sardanapalus* and the *Two Foscari* enlisted also the fervor of this actor's dramatic indorsement. But these all—needed a Macready.

Out of the Venetian welter came, too, the fourth canto of *Childe Harold* and the opening parts of *Don Juan.* The mocking, rollicking, marvellous *Vision of Judgment,* whose daring license staggered even Murray and Moore, and which scarified poor Southey, belongs to a later phase of his Italian career. It is angry and bitter — and has an impish laughter in it — of a sort which our friend Robert Ingersoll might write, if his genius ran to poetry. *Cain* had been of a bolder tone — perhaps loftier ; with much of the argument that Milton puts into the mouth of Satan, amplified and rounded, and the whole illuminated by passages of wonderful poetic beauty.

His scepticism, if not so out-spoken and full of plump negatives as that of Shelley, is far more mocking and bitter. If Shelley was rich in negations — so far as relates to orthodox belief — he was also rich in dim, shadowy conceptions of a mysterious eternal region, with faith and love reigning in it — toward which in his highest range of poetic effusion he makes approaches with an awed and a tremulous step. But with Byron —

even where his words carry full theistic beliefs — the awe and the tremulous approaches are wanting.

Shelley Again.

Shelley went back from Switzerland to a home for a year or more, beyond Windsor, near to Bisham — amid some of the loveliest country that borders upon the Thames. Here he wrote that strange poem of *Laon and Cythna* (or *Revolt of Islam*, as it was called on its re-issue), which, so far as one can gather meaning from its redundant and cumulated billows of rich, poetic language, tells how a nation was kindled to freedom by the strenuous outcry of some young poet-prophet — how he seems to win, and his enemies become like smoking flax — how the dreadful fates that beset us, and crowd all worldly courses from their best outcome, did at last trample him down; not him only, but the one dearest to him — who is a willing victim — and bears him off into the shades of night. Throughout, Laon the Victim is the poet's very self; and the very self appears again — with what seems to the cautious, world-wise reader

IV.—15

a curious indiscretion — in the pretty jumping metre of " Rosalind and Helen " :—

> " Joyous he was; and hope and peace
> On all who heard him did abide,
> Raining like dew from his sweet talk,
> As where the evening star may walk
> Along the brink of the gloomy seas,
> Liquid mists of splendid quiver.
> His very gestures touched to tears
> The unpersuaded tyrant, never
> So moved before. . . .
> Men wondered, and some sneered, to see
> One sow what he could never reap;
> For he is rich, they said, and young,
> And might drink from the depths of luxury.
> If he seeks Fame, Fame never crowned
> The champion of a trampled creed;
> If he seeks Power, Power is enthroned
> 'Mid ancient rights and wrongs, to feed
> Which hungry wolves with praise and spoil,
> Those who would sit near Power must toil."

It was in 1818, four years before his death, that Shelley sailed away from English shores forever. There was not much to hold him there ; those children of the Westbrook mother he cannot know or guide.* The Chancellor of England has decided

---

* Very full account of the Chancery proceedings in respect to children of Shelley may be found in Professor Dowden's

that question against him ; and Law, which he has defied, has wrought him this great pain ; nay, he has wild, imaginary fears, too, that some Lord Chancellor, weaving toils in that web of orderly British custom, may put bonds on these other and younger children of the Godwin blood. Nor is it strange that a world of more reasonable motives should urge this subtle poet — whose head is carried of purpose, and by love, among the clouds — to turn his back on that grimy, matter-of-fact England, and set his face toward those southern regions where Art makes daily food, and where he may trail his robes without the chafings of law or custom. But do not let me convey the impression that Shelley then or ever lived day by day wantonly lawless, or doing violence to old-fashioned proprieties ; drunkenness was always a stranger to him, to that new household — into which he had been grafted by Godwinian ethics — he is normally true ; he would, if it were possible, bring

biography. By this it would appear that by decision of Lord Eldon (July 25, 1818) Shelley was allowed to see his children twelve times a year — if in the presence of their regularly appointed guardians (Dr. and Mrs. Hume).

into the lap of his charities those other estrays
from whom the law divides him ; his generosities
are of the noblest and fullest ; he even entertains
at one time the singular caprice of "taking
orders," as if the author of *Queen Mab* could hold
a vicarage ! It opens, he said, so many ways of
doing kindly things, of making hearts joyful ; and
— for doctrine, one can always preach Charity !
With rare exceptions, it is only in his mental attitudes and forays that he oversteps the metes and
bounds of the every-day moralities around him.
Few poets, even of that time, can or do so measure
him as to enjoy him or to give him joy. Leigh
Hunt is gracious and kindly ; but there are no
winged sandals on his feet which can carry him
into regions where Shelley walks. Southey is
stark unbeliever in the mystic fields where Shelley
grazes. Wordsworth is conquered by the Art, but
has melancholy doubts of the soul that seems
caught and hindered in the meshes of its own
craftsmanship. Landor, of a certainty, has de-
tected with his keen insight the high faculties
that run rampant under the mazes of the new
poet's language ; but Landor, too, is in exile—

driven hither and thither by the same lack of steady home affinities which has overset and embroiled the domesticities of the younger poet.

John Keats.

Yet another singer of these days, in most earnest sympathy with the singing moods of Shelley — for whom I can have only a word now, was John Keats ; * born within the limits of London smoke, and less than three-quarters of a mile from London Bridge — knowing in his boy days only the humblest, work-a-day ranges of life ; getting some good Latinity and other schooling out of a Mr. Clarke (of the Cowden Clarke family) — reading Virgil with him, but no Greek. And yet the lad, who never read Homer save in Chapman, when he comes to write, as he does in extreme youth, crowds his wonderful lines with the delicate trills and warblings which might have broken out straight from Helicon — with a susurrus from the Bees of Hymettus. This makes a good argument

---

* John Keats, b. 1795; d. 1821. First " collected " *Poems,* 1817; *Endymion,* 1818; second volume of collected *Poems,* 1820; *Life and Letters* — Lord Houghton (Milnes), 1848.

— so far as it reaches — in disproof of the aver-
ments of those who believe that, for conquest of
Attic felicities of expression, the Greek vocables
must needs be torn forth root by root, and
stretched to dry upon our skulls.

He published *Endymion* in the very year when
Shelley set off on his final voyagings — a gushing,
wavy, wandering poem, intermeshed with flowers
and greenery (which he lavishes), and with fairy
golden things in it and careering butterflies ; with
some bony under-structure of Greek fable — loose
and vague — and serving only as the caulking pins
to hold together the rich, sensuous sway, and the
temper and roll of his language.

I must snatch one little bit from that book of
Endymion, were it only to show you what music
was breaking out in unexpected quarters from that
fact-ridden England, within sound of the murmurs
of the Thames, when Shelley was sailing away :—

> " On every morrow are we wreathing
> A flowery band to bind us to the earth
> Spite of despondence, of the inhuman dearth
> Of noble natures, of the gloomy days,
> Of all the unhealthy and o'er-darkened ways
> Made for our searching; yes, in spite of all,

Some shape of beauty moves away the pall
From our dark spirits. Such — the sun, the moon,
Trees — old and young, sprouting a shady boon
For simple sheep; and such are daffodils
With the green world they live in; and clear rills
That for themselves a cooling covert make
'Gainst the hot season; the mid-forest brake
Rich with a sprinkling of fair musk-rose blooms;
And such, too, is the grandeur of the dooms
We have imagined for the mighty dead;
All lovely tales that we have heard or read."

I might cite page on page from Keats, and yet
hold your attention; there is something so beguiling in his witching words; and his pictures are
finished — with only one or two or three dashes of
his pencil. Thus we come upon —

"Swelling downs, where sweet air stirs
Blue harebells lightly, and where prickly furze
Buds lavish gold."

And again our ear is caught with —

"Rustle of the reapéd corn,
And sweet birds antheming the morn."

Well, this young master of song goes to Italy,
too — not driven, like Byron, by hue and cry, or
like Shelley, restless for change (from Chancellor's
courts) and for wider horizons — but running from
the disease which has firm grip upon him, and

which some three years after Shelley's going
kills the poet of the *Endymion* at Rome. His
ashes lie in the Protestant burial-ground there—
under the shadow of the pyramid of Caius Cestius.
Every literary traveller goes to see the grave, and
to spell out the words he wanted inscribed there :

"Here lies one whose name was writ in water."

Upon that death, Shelley, then living in Pisa,
blazed out in the *Adonais*—the poem making,
with the *Lycidas* of Milton, and the *In Memoriam*
of Tennyson, a triplet of laurel garlands, whose
leaves will never fade. Yet those of Shelley have
a cold rustle in them—shine as they may :—

" Oh, weep for Adonais — he is dead!
 Wake, melancholy mother, wake and weep!
Yet wherefore? Quench within their burning bed
 Thy fiery tears, and let thy loud heart keep
 Like his — a mute and uncomplaining sleep.
For he is gone where all things wise and fair
 Descend. Oh, dream not that the amorous deep
Will yet restore him to the vital air;
Death feeds on his mute voice and laughs at our despair.

" Oh, weep for Adonais! The quick dreams,
 The passion-winged ministers of thought
Who were his flocks, whom near the living streams

Of his young spirit he fed, and whom he taught
The Love which was its music, wander not —
Wander no more from kindling brain to brain,
But droop there whence they sprung; and mourn their lot
Round the cold heart, where, after their sweet pain,
They ne'er will gather strength, or find a home again."

The weak place in this impassioned commemorative poem lies in its waste of fire upon the heads of those British critics, who — as flimsy, pathetic legends used to run — slew the poet by their savagery. Keats did not range among giants; but he was far too strong a man to die of the gibes of the *Quarterly,* or the jeers of *Blackwood.* Not this; but all along, throughout his weary life — even amid the high airs of Hampstead, where nightingales sang — he sang, too,—

" I have been half in love with easeful Death,
    Called him soft names in many a muséd rhyme,
    To take into the air my quiet breath." *

Buried in Rome.

Keats died in 1821. In that year Shelley was living between Lirici, on the gulf of Spezia, and Pisa. While in this latter city, he was planted for

---

* " Ode to a Nightingale," vi.

a time at the old Lanfranchi palace, where in the
following season very much at the instance and
urgence of Shelley, Leigh Hunt came with his six
riotous young children, and sometimes made a din
— that was new to Byron and most worrisome —
in the court of the Lanfranchi house.   Out of this
Hunt fraternizing and co-working (forecast by the
kindly Shelley) was to be built up the success of
that famous "Liberal" Journal, dear to the hearts
of Shelley and Hunt, of which I have already
spoken, and which had disastrous failure; out of
this aggregation of disorderly poetic elements grew
also the squabbles that gave such harsh color to
the *Reminiscences* of Leigh Hunt.*

But other and graver disaster was impending.
Shelley loved the sea, and carried with him to the
water the same reckless daring which he put into
his verse.   Upon a summer day of July, 1822, he
went with a friend and one boatman for a sail
upon the bay of Spezia, not heeding some cau-

---

* In letter 573, to Murray (Halleck Col., date of Genoa,
November, 1822), Byron says : " I see somebody represents
the Hunts and Mrs. Shelley as living in my house; it is a
falsehood. . . . I do not see them twice a month."

tions that had been dropped by old seamen, who
had seen portents of a storm; and his boat sailed
away into the covert of the clouds. Next day
there were no tidings, nor the next, nor the next.
Finally wreck and bodies came to the shore.

Trelawney, Byron's friend, tells a grim story of
it all — how the dismal truth was carried to the
widowed wife, how the body of the drowned poet
was burned upon the shore, with heathen libations
of oil and wine; how Byron and Hunt both were
present at the weird funeral — the blue Mediterranean lapping peacefully upon the beach and the
black smoke lifting in great clouds from the pyre
and throwing lurid shadows over the silent company. The burial — such as there was of it — took
place in that same Protestant graveyard at Rome
— just out of the Porta San Paolo — where we
were just now witnesses at the burial of Keats.

Shelley made many friendships, and lasting
ones. He was wonderfully generous; he visited
the sick; he helped the needy; putting himself
often into grievous straits for means to give
quickly. As he was fine of figure and of feature,
so his voice was fine, delicate, penetrative, yet in

moments of great excitement rising to a shrillness that spoiled melody and rasped the ear; so his finer generosities and kindnesses sometimes passed into a rasping indifference or even cruelty toward those nearest him, he feeling that first West-brook *mesalliance,* on occasions, like a torture — specially when the presence of the tyrannic, coarse, aggravating sister-in-law was like a poi-sonous irritant; he — under the teachings of a conscientious father, in his young days — was scarce more than half responsible for his wry life; running to badnesses — on occasions — under good impulses; perhaps marrying that first wife because she wanted to marry him; and quitting her — well — because "she didn't care." Intel-lectually, as well as morally, he was pagan; seeing things in their simplest aspects, and so dealing with them; intense, passionate, borne away in tempests of quick decision, whose grounds he cannot fathom; always beating his wings against the cagements that hem us in; eager to look into those depths where light is blinding and will not let us look; seeming at times to measure by some sudden reach of soul what is immeasurable; but

under the vain uplifts, always reverent, with a dim
hope shining fitfully; contemptuous of harassing
creeds or any jugglery of forms — of whatever
splendid fashionings of mere material, whether
robes or rites — and yearning to solve by some
strong, swift flight of imagination what is insolu-
ble. There are many reverent steps that go to
that little Protestant cemetery — an English
greenery upon the borders of the Roman Cam-
pagna — where the ashes of Shelley rest and
where myrtles grow. And from its neighborhood, between Mount Aventine and the Janiculan
heights, one may see reaches of the gleaming
Tiber, and the great dome of St. Peter's lifting
against the northern sky, like another tomb, its
cross almost hidden in the gray distance.

Pisa and Don Juan.

No such friendship as that whose gleams have
shot athwart these latter pages could have been
kindled by Byron. No "Adonais" could have
been writ for him; he could have melted into no
"Adonais" for another; old pirate blood, seething
in him, forbade. No wonder he chafed at Hunt's

squalling children in the Lanfranchi palace; *that* literary partnership finds quick dissolution. He sees on rare occasions an old English friend — he, who has so few! Yet he is in no mood to make new friends. The lambent flames of the Guiccioli romance hover and play about him, making the only counterfeit of a real home which he has ever known. The proud, independent, audacious, lawless living that has been his so long, whether the early charms lie in it or no — he still clings by. His pen has its old force, and the words spin from it in fiery lines; but to pluck the flowers worth the seeking, which he plants in them now, one must go over quaking bogs, and through ways of foulness.

The *Childe Harold* has been brought to its conclusion long before; its cantos, here and there splendidly ablaze with Nature — its storms, its shadows, its serenities; and the sentiment — now morbid, now jubilant — is always his own, though it beguiles with honeyed sounds, or stabs like a knife.

There have been a multitude of lesser poems, and of dramas which have had their inception

and their finish on that wild Continental holiday
— beginning on *Lac Leman* and ending at Pisa
and Genoa; but his real selfhood — whether of
mind or passion — seems to me to come out plain-
er and sharper in the *Don Juan* than elsewhere.
There may not be lifts in it, which rise to the romantic levels of the "Pilgrimage;" there may
be lack of those interpolated bits of passion, of
gloom, of melancholy, which break into the
earlier poem. But there is the blaze and crackle
of his own mad march of flame; the soot, the cin-
ders, the heat, the wide-spread ashes, and unrest
of those fires which burned in him from the begin-
ing were there, and devastated all the virginal
purities of his youth (if indeed there were any!)
and welded his satanic and his poetic qualities into
that seamy, shining, wonderful residue of dirty
scoriæ, and of brilliant phosphorescence, which we
call *Don Juan*. From a mere literary point of
view there are trails of doggerel in it, which the
poet was too indolent to mend, and too proud to
exclude. Nor can it ever be done; a revised
Byron would be not only a Byron emasculated,
but decapitated and devastated. 'Twould lack the

links that tie it to the humanities which coil and
writhe tortuously all up and down his pages. His
faults of prosody, or of ethics, or of facts — his
welter, at intervals, through a barren splendor of
words — are all typical of that fierce, proud, un-
governable, unconventional nature. This leopard
will and should carry all his spots. We cannot
shrive the man ; no chanters or churches can do
this ; he disdains to be shriven at human hands,
or, it would seem, any other hands. The impact
of that strong, vigorous nature — through his
poems — brings, to the average reader, a sense of
force, of brilliancy, of personality, of humanity (if
gone astray), which exhilarates, which dashes away
a thousand wordy memories of wordy verses, and
puts in their place palpitating phrases that throb
with life. An infinite capability for eloquent
verse ; an infinite capability for badnesses ! We
cannot root out the satanry from the man, or his
books, any more than we can root out Lucifer
from Milton's Eden. But we can lament both,
and, if need be, fight them.

Whether closer British influence (which usually
smote upon him, like sleet on glass) — even of

that "Ancient Oratory" of Annesley — would have served to whiten his tracks, who shall say? Long ago he had gone out from them, and from parish church and sermon; his hymns were the *Ranz des Vaches* on the heights of the *Dent de Jaman*, and the preachments he heard were the mellowed tones of convent bells — filtering through forest boughs — maybe upon the ear of some hapless Allegra, scathed by birth-marks of a sin that is not her own — conning her beads, and listening and praying!

Missolonghi.

It was in 1823, when he was living in Genoa — whither he had gone from Pisa (and before this, Ravenna) — that his sympathies were awakened in behalf of the Greeks, who since 1820 had been in revolt against their Turkish taskmasters. He had been already enrolled with those Carbonari — the forerunners of the Mazzinis and the Garibaldis — who had labored in vain for the independence and unity of Italy; and in many a burst of his impassioned song he had showered welcoming praises

IV.—16

upon a Greece that should be free, and with equal passion attuned his verse to the lament — that

" Freedom found no champion and no child
    Such as Columbia saw arise when she
    Sprung forth a Pallas, armed and undefiled."

How much all this was real and how much only the romanticism of the poet, was now to be proven.   And it was certainly with a business-like air that he cut short his little *agaceries* with the Lady Blessington, and pleasant dalliance with the Guiccioli, for a rallying of all his forces — moneyed or other — in the service of that cause for which the brave Marco Bozzaris had fallen, fighting, only three months before.   It was in July that he embarked at Genoa for Greece — in a brig which he had chartered, and which took guns and ammunition and $40,000 of his own procurement, with a retinue of attendants — including his trusty Fletcher — besides his friends Trelawney and the Count Gamba.   They skirted the west coast of Italy, catching sight of Elba — then famous for its Napoleonic associations — and of Stromboli, whose lurid blaze, reflected upon the sea, startled the admiring poet to a hinted promise — that those fires should upon some near day reek on the pages of a Fifth Canto of *Childe Harold.*

Mediterranean ships were slow sailers in those days, and it was not until August that they arrived and disembarked at Cephalonia — an island near to the outlet of the Gulf of Corinth, and lying due east from the Straits of Messina. There was a boisterous welcome to the generous and eloquent peer of England ; but it was a welcome that showed factional discords. Only across a mile or two of water lay the Isle of Ithaca, full of vague, Homeric traditions, which under other conditions he would have been delighted to follow up ; but the torturing perplexities about the distribution of moneys or ammunition, the jealousies of quarrelsome chieftains, the ugly watch over drafts and bills of exchange, and the griping exactions of local money-changers, made all Homeric fancies or memories drift away with the scuds of wind that blew athwart the Ionian seas.

He battled bravely with the cumulating difficulties — sometimes maddened to regret — other times lifted to enthusiasm by the cordial greeting of such a chieftain as Mavrocordatos, or the street

cheers of a band of Suliotes. So months passed,
until he embarked again, in equipage of his own,
with his own fittings, for Missolonghi, where
final measures were to be taken. Meantime he is
paying for his ships, paying for his Suliotes,
paying for delays, and beset by rival chieftains for
his interest, or his stimulating presence, or his
more stimulating moneys. On this new but short
sea venture he barely escapes capture by a Turkish frigate — is badly piloted among the rocky
islets which stud the shores; suffers grievous
exposure — coming at last, wearied and weakened,
to a new harborage, where welcomes are vocif-
erous, but still wofully discordant. He labors
wearily to smooth the troubled waters, his old,
splendid allegiance to a free and united Greece
suffering grievous quakes, and doubts; and when
after months of alternating turbulence and rest
there seems promise of positive action, he is
smitten by the fever of those low coasts — aggra-
vated by his always wanton exposures. The attack
is as sudden as a shot from a gun — under
which he staggers and falls, writhing with pain,
and I know not what convulsional agonies.

There is undertaken an Italian regimen of cupping and leeching about the brow and temples, from which the bleeding is obstinate, and again and again renewed. But he rallies ; attendants are assiduous in their care. Within a day or two he has recovered much of the old *vires vitæ*, when on a sudden there is an alarm ; a band of mutinous Suliotes, arms in hand, break into his lordship's apartments, madly urging some trumpery claim for back-pay. Whereupon Byron — showing the old savagery of his ancestors — leaps from his bed, seizes whatever weapon is at hand, and gory — with his bandaged head still trickling blood — he confronts the mutineers ; his strength for the moment is all his own again, and they are cowered into submission, their yataghans clinking as they drop to the tiled flooring of his room.

'Twas a scene for Benjamin West to have painted in the spirit of Death on the Pale Horse, or for some later artist — loving bloody "impressions." However, peace is established. Quiet reigns once more (we count by days only, now). There is a goodly scheme for attack upon the fortress which guards the Gulf of Lepanto (Cor-

inth) ; the time is set ; the guards are ready ;
the Suliotes are under bidding ; the chieftains are
(for once) agreed, when, on the 18th, he falters,
sinks, murmurs some last words — "Ada —
daughter — love — Augusta —" barely caught ;
doubtfully caught ; but it is all — and the poet
of *Childe Harold* is gone, and that turbulent,
brilliant career hushed in night.

It was on April 19, 1824, that he died. His
body was taken home for burial. I said *home ;*
'twere better to have said to England, to the
family vault, in which his mother had been laid ;
and at a later day, his daughter, Ada, was buried
there beside him, in the old Hucknall-Torkard
church. The building is heavy and bald, without
the winning picturesqueness that belongs to so
many old country churches of Yorkshire. The beatitudes that are intoned under its timbered arch
are not born of any rural beatitudes in the surroundings. The town is small, straggly, bricky,*
and neither church nor hamlet nor neighbors'

---

* Professor Hoppin, in his honest and entertaining *Old
England*, speaks of it (p. 258) as "a dull, dirty village," and
— of the church — as "most forlorn."

houses arc suffused with those softened tints which
verdure, and nice keeping, and mellow sunshine
give to so many villages of southern England.
Hucknall-Torkard is half way between Nottingham and Newstead, and lies upon that northern
road which pushes past Annesley into the region
of woods and parks where Sherwood forest once
flung its shadows along the aisles in which the
bugle notes of master Robin Hood woke the echoes.

But Hucknall-Torkard church is bald and tame.
Mr. Winter, in his pleasant descriptive sketch,*
does indeed give a certain glow to the "grim"
tower, and many a delightful touch to the gray
surroundings; but even he would inhibit the
pressure of the noisy market-folk against the
churchyard walls, and their rollicking guffaw.
And yet, somehow, the memory of Byron does
not seem to me to mate well with either home or
church quietudes, and their serenities. Is it not
proper and fitting after all that the clangor of a
rebellious and fitful world should voice itself near
such a grave? Old mossy and ivied towers in

---

* *Gray Days and Gold;* chapter viii. Macmillan, 1896.

which church bells are a-chime, and near trees
where rooks are cawing with home-sounds, do not
marry happily with our memories of Byron.

Best of all if he had been given burial where
his heart lies, in that Ætolian country, upon some
shaggy fore-land from which could have been seen
— one way, Ithaca and the Ionian seas, and to
the southward, across the Straits of Lepanto, the
woody depths of the Morea, far as Arcadia.

But there is no mending the matter now; he
lies beside his harsh Gordon mother in the middle
of the flat country of stockings, lace curtains, and
collieries.

Another poet, William Lisle Bowles, in a quaint
sonnet has versed this Gordon mother's imaginary
welcome to her dead son :—

> " Could that mother speak,
> In thrilling, but with hollow accent weak,
> She thus might give the welcome of the dead :
> ' Here rest, my son, with me ; the dream is fled ;
> The motley mask, and the great stir is o'er.
> Welcome to me, and to this silent bed,
> Where deep forgetfulness succeeds the roar
> Of life, and fretting passions waste the heart no more !' "

CHAPTER VII.

FOR many a page now we have spoken inter-
mittently of that extraordinary man and
poet — full of power and full of passion, both
uncontrolled — whose surroundings we found in
that pleasantly undulating Nottingham country
where Newstead Abbey piled above its lawn and
its silent tarns — half a ruin, and half a home.*
Nor did Byron ever know a home which showed
no ruin — nor ever know a ruin, into which his
verse did not nestle as into a home.

We traced him from the keeping of that passionate mother — who smote him through and through

---

* This relates, of course, to the condition of the Abbey in
the days of Byron's childhood. Colonel Wildman, a distinguished officer in the Peninsular War, who succeeded to
the ownership (by purchase) about 1817, expended very
large sums upon such judicious improvements as took away
its old look of desolation.

249

with her own wrathful spirit — to the days when
he uttered the "Idle" songs — coined in the courts
of Cambridge — and to those quick succeeding
days, when his mad verse maddened English bards
and Scotch reviewers. Then came the passages of
love — with Mary Chaworth, which was real and
vain ; with a Milbanke, which was a mockery and
ended in worse than mockery ; all these experiences whetting the edge of that sword of song
with which he carved a road of romance for thou-
sands of after journeymen to travel, through
the old Iberian Peninsula, and the vales of Thessaly. Then there was the turning away, in rage,
from the shores of England, the episode with the
Shelley household on the borders of Lake Leman,
with its record of "crag-splitting" storms and
sunny siestas ; and such enduring memorials as
the ghastly *Frankenstein* of Mrs. Shelley, the
Third Canto of *Childe Harold*, and the child-
name of — Allegra.

Next came Venice, where the waves lapped
murmurously upon the door-steps of the palaces
which "Mi-lord" made noisy with his audacious
revelry. To this succeeded the long stay at Ra-

venna, with its pacifying and lingering, reposeful reach of an attachment, which was beautiful in its sincerity, but as lawless as his life. After Ravenna came Pisa with its Hunt-Lanfranchi coruscations of spleen, and its weird interlude of the burning of the body of his poor friend Shelley upon the Mediterranean shores. Song, and drama, and tender verselets, and bagnio-tainted pictures of Don Juan, gleamed with fervid intensity through the interstices of this Italian life; but they all came to a sudden stay when he sailed for Greece, and with a generosity as strong as his wilder passions, flung away his fortune and his life in that vortex of Suliote strifes and deadly miasmas, which was centred amid the swamp-lands of Missolonghi.

The Cretans of to-day (1897), and the men of Thessaly, and of the Morea, and Albanians all, may find a lift of their ambitions and a spur to their courage in Byron's sacrifice to their old struggle for liberty, and in his magnificent outburst of patriotic song. So, too, those who love real poetry will never cease to admire his subtle turns of thought, and his superb command of all the resources of language. But the households are few in which his name will be revered as an apostle of those cheering altitudes of thought which encourage high endeavor, or of those tenderer humanities which spur to kindly deeds, and give their glow to the atmosphere of homes.

King William's Time.

The last figure that we dealt with among England's kings was that bluff, vulgar-toned sailor, William IV., whom even the street-folk criticise, because he spat from his carriage window when driving on some State ceremonial.* Nor was this the worst of his coarsenesses ; he swore — with great ease and pungency. He forgot his dignity ; he insulted his ministers ; he gave to Queen Adelaide, who survived him many years as dowager, many most uncomfortable half-hours ; and if he read the new sea-stories of Captain Marryat — though he read very little — I suspect he loved

---

* *Croker Papers*, chapter xviii. Closing of Session of 1833. Croker would have spoken more gently of him in those latter days, when the king turned his back on Reformers.

more the spicier condiments of *Peregrine Pickle* and of *Tom Jones.*

Yet during the period of his short reign — scarce seven years — events happened — some through his slow helpfulness, and none suffering grievously from his obstructiveness — which gave new and brighter color to the political development and to the literary growth of England. There was, for instance, the passage of the Reform Bill of 1832 (of which I have already spoken, in connection with Sydney Smith) — not indeed accomplishing all its friends had hoped ; not inaugurating a political millennium ; not doing away with the harsh frictions of state-craft ; no reforms ever do or can ; but broadening the outlook and range of all publicists, and stirring quiet thinkers into aggressive and kindling and hopeful speech. Very shortly after this followed the establishment of that old society for the "Diffusion of Useful Knowledge" which came soon to the out-put — under the editorship of Charles Knight — of the *Penny Cyclopædia* and the *Penny Magazine.**

* The *Penny Magazine* appeared first in 1832 ; the *Cyclopædia* in the following year.

I recall distinctly the delight with which — as boys — we lingered over the pictured pages of that magazine — the great forerunner of all of our illustrated monthlies.

To the same period belong those *Tracts for the Times*, in which John Keble, the honored author of the *Christian Year*, came to new notice, while his associates, Dr. Pusey and Cardinal Newman, gave utterance to speech which is not without reverberating echoes, even now. Nor was it long after this date that British journalism received a great lift, and a great broadening of its forces, by a reduction of the stamp-tax — largely due to the efforts of Bulwer Lytton — whereby British newspapers increased their circulation, within two years, by 20,000,000 annually.*

All these things had come about in the reign of William IV. ; but to none of them had he given any enthusiastic approval, or any such urgence of attention as would have dislocated a single one of his royal dinners.

In 1837 he died — not very largely sighed over ;

---

* The reduction of tax from 4*d.* to 1*d.* took place in 1836.

least of all by that sister-in-law, the Duchess of Kent, whom he had hated for her starched proprieties, whom he had insulted again and again, and who now, in her palace of Kensington, prepared her daughter Victoria for her entrance upon the sovereignty.

Her Majesty Victoria.

The girl was only eighteen — well taught, discreet, and modest. Greville tells us that she was consumed with blushes when her uncles of Sussex and of Cumberland came, with the royal council, to kneel before her, and to kiss her hand in token of the new allegiance.

The old king had died at two o'clock of the morning; and by eleven o'clock on the same day the duties of royalty had begun for the young queen, in receiving the great officers of state. Among the others she meets on that first regal day in Kensington Palace, are Lansdowne, the fidgety Lord Brougham, the courtly Sir Robert Peel, and the spare, trim-looking old Duke of Wellington, who is charmed by her gracious manner, and by her self-control and dignity. He said he could not have been more proud of her if she had been his own daughter.

Nearer to the young queen than all these — by old ties of friendship, that always remained unshaken — was the suave and accomplished Lord Melbourne — First Minister — who has prepared the queen's little speech for her, which she reads with charming self-possession ; to him, too, she looks for approval and instruction in all her progress through the new ceremonials of Court, and the ordering of a royal household. And Melbourne is admirably suited to that task ; he was not a great statesman ; was never an orator, but possessed of all the arts of conciliation — adroit and full of tact, yet kindly, sympathetic, and winning. Not by any means a man beyond reproach in his private life, but bringing to those new offices of political guardianship to the young queen only the soundest good - sense and the wisest of advice — thus inspiring in her a trust that was never forfeited.

Indeed, it was under Melbourne's encouragements, and his stimulative commendation (if stimulus were needed), that the young princess formed shortly after that marriage relation which proved altogether a happy one — giving to England and to the world shining proof that righteous domesticities were not altogether clean gone from royal houses. And if the good motherly rulings have not had their best issues with some of the male members of the family, can we not match these wry tendencies with those fastening upon the boys of well-ordered households all around us? It is not in royal circles only that his satanic majesty makes friends of nice boys, when the girls escape him — or seem to !

Well, I have gone back to that old palace of Kensington, which still, with its mossy brick walls, in the west of London, baffles the years, and the fogs — the same palace where we went to find William III. dying, and the gracious Queen Anne too ; and where now the Marquis of Lorne and the Princess Louise have their home. I have taken you again there to see how the young Victoria bore herself at the news of her accession — with the great councillors of the kingdom about her — not alone because those whom we shall bring to the front, in this closing chapter, have wrought

IV.—17

during her reign ; but because, furthermore,
she with her household have been encouragers
and patrons of both letters and of art in many
most helpful ways ; and yet, again, because this
queen, who has within this twelvemonth (1897)
made her new speech to Parliament — sixty years
after that first little speech at Kensington — is
herself, in virtue of certain modest book-making,
to be enrolled with all courtesy in the Guild of
Letters.   And though the high-stepping critics
may be inclined to question the literary judgment
or the scrupulous finish of her book-work, we cannot, I think, deny to it a thoroughly humane tone,
and a tender realism.   We greet her not only by
reason of her queenship proper, but for that larger
sovereignty of womanhood and of motherhood
which she has always dignified and adorned.

I once caught such glimpse of her — as strangers
may — in the flush of her early wedded life ; not
beautiful surely, but comely, kindly, and radiant,
in the enjoyment of — what is so rare with sover-
eigns — a happy home - life ; and again I came
upon other sight of her eight years later, when
the prince was a rollicking boy, and the princess a

blooming maiden ; these and lesser rosy-cheeked ones were taking the air on the terrace at Windsor, almost in the shadow of the great keep, which has frowned there since the days of Edward III.

Macaulay.

In the early days of Queen Victoria's reign — when Sir Robert Peel was winning his way to the proud position he later held — when American and English politicians were getting into the toils of the " Maine Boundary " dispute (afterward settled by Ashburton and Webster), and when the Countess of Blessington was making " Gore House " lively with her little suppers, and the banker Rogers entertaining all *beaux esprits* at his home near the Green Park, there may have been found as guest at one of the banker's famous breakfasts — somewhere we will say in the year 1838 — a man, well - preserved, still under forty — with a shaggy brow, with clothes very likely ill-adjusted and ill-fitting, and with gloves which are never buttoned — who has just come back from India, where he has held lucrative official position. He is cogitating, it is said, a history of England, and his talk has a fulness and richness that seem inexhaustible.

You know to whom I must refer — Thomas Babington Macaulay * — not a new man at Rogers's table, not a new man to bookish people; for he had won his honors in literature, especially by a first paper on Milton, published in the year 1825 in the *Edinburgh Review.* This bore a new stamp and had qualities that could not be overlooked. There are scores of us who read that paper for the first time in the impressionable days of youth, who are carried back now by the mere mention of it to the times of the old Puritan poet.

"We can almost fancy that we are visiting him in his small lodging; that we see him sitting at the old organ beneath the faded green hangings; that we can catch the quick twinkle of his eyes, rolling in vain to find the day; that we are reading in the lines of his noble countenance the proud and mournful history of his glory and his affliction!"

Macaulay came of good old Scotch stock — his forefathers counting up patriarchal families in

* Thomas Babington Macaulay, b. 1800; d. 1859. *History of England*, 1848-55-61. *Lays of Ancient Rome*, 1842. His *Essays* (published in America), 1840. Complete *Works*, London, 8 vols., 1866. *Life*, by Trevelyan, 1876.

Coll and Inverary; but his father, Zachary Macaulay, well known for his anti-slavery action and influence, and for his association with Wilberforce, married an English Quaker girl from Bristol — said to have been a *protégée* of our old friend, Mistress Hannah More. Of this marriage was born, in 1800, at the charming country house of an aunt, named Babington, in the pleasant county of Leicestershire, the future historian.

The father's first London home was near by Lombard Street, where he managed an African agency under the firm name of Macaulay & Babington; and the baby Macaulay used to be wheeled into an open square near by, for the enjoyment of such winter's sunshine as fell there at far-away intervals. His boyish memories, however, belonged to a later home at Clapham, then a suburban village. There, was his first schooling, and there he budded out — to the wonderment of all his father's guests — into young poems and the drollest of precocious talk. His pleasant biographer (Trevelyan) tells of a visit the bright boy made at Strawberry Hill — Walpole's old showplace. There was a spilling of hot drink of some

sort, during the visitation, which came near to
scalding the lad ; and when the sympathizing
hostess asked after his suffering : " Thank you,
madam," said he, " the agony is abated ! " The
story is delightfully credible ; and so are other
pleasant ones of his reciting some of his doggerel
verses to Hannah More and getting a gracious and
approving nod of her gray curls and of her mob-
cap.

At Cambridge, where he went at the usual student age, he studied what he would, and discarded
what he would — as he did all through his life.
For mathematics he had a distinguished repug-
nance, then and always ; and if brought to task
by them in those student days — trying hard to
twist their certainties into probabilities, and so
make them subject to that world of "ifs and
buts" which he loved to start buzzing about the
ears of those who loved the exact sciences better
than he. He missed thus some of the University
honors, it is true ; yet, up and down in those Cambridge coteries he was a man looked for, and listened to, eagerly and bravely applauded. Certain
scholastic honors, too, he did reap, in spite of his

lunges outside the traces; there was a medal for
his poem of *Pompeii*; and a Fellowship, at last,
which gave him a needed, though small income —
his father's Afric business having proved a failure,
and no home moneys coming to him thereafter.

The first writings of Macaulay which had public
issue were printed in *Knight's Quarterly Magazine* — among them were criticisms on Italian
writers, a remarkable imaginary conversation between "Cowley and Milton," and the glittering,
jingling battle verses about the War of the
League and stout "Henry of Navarre" — full to
the brim of that rush and martial splendor which
he loved all his life, and which he brought in later
years to his famous re-heralding of the *Lays of
Ancient Rome.* A few lines are cited:—

" The King is come to marshal us, in all his armor drest;
And he has bound a snow-white plume upon his gallant crest.
He looked upon his people, and a tear was in his eye;
He looked upon the traitors, and his glance was stern and
　　high.
Right graciously he smiled on us, as rolled from wing to
　　wing
Down all our line a deafening shout, ' God save our Lord
　　the King ! '

And if my standard bearer fall, as fall full well he may,
For never saw I promise yet of such a bloody fray;
Press where ye see my white plume shine, amidst the ranks
    of war,
And be your oriflamme to-day the helmet of Navarre!"

On the year after this "Battle of Ivry" had
sparkled into print appeared the paper on Milton, to which I have alluded, and which straightway set London doors open to the freshly
fledged student-at-law. Crabb Robinson, in his
diary of those days, speaks patronizingly of a
"young gentleman of six or seven and twenty,
who has emerged upon the dinner-giving public,"
and is astounding old habitués by his fulness and
brilliancy of talk. He had not, to be sure, those
lighter and sportive graces of conversation which
floated shortly thereafter out from the open windows of Gore House, and had burgeoned under the
beaming smiles of Lady Blessington. But he
came to be a table match for Sydney Smith, and
was honored by the invitations of Lady Holland.*

---

* Greville (*Journal of Queen Victoria's Time*, vol. i., p.
369) speaks of a dinner at Lady Holland's — Macaulay being
present — when her ladyship, growing tired of the eloquence

who allowed no new find of so brilliant feather to escape her.

In Politics and Verse.

Macaulay's alliance with the Scottish Reviewers, and his known liberalism, make him a pet of the great Whigs ; and through Lansdowne, with a helping hand from Melbourne, he found his way into Parliament : there were those who prophesied his failure in that field ; I think Brougham in those days, with not a little of jealousy in his make up, was disposed to count him a mere essayist. But his speeches in favor of the Reform bill belied all such auguries. Sir Robert Peel declared them to be wonderful in their grasp and eloquence ; they certainly had great weight in furthering reform ; and his parliamentary work won presently for him the offer from Government of a place in India. No Oriental glamour allured him, but the new position was worth £10,000 per annum. He counted

---

of Speakers of the House of Commons and Fathers of the Church, said : " Well, Mr. Macaulay, can you tell us anything of dolls — when first named or used? " Macaulay was ready on the instant — dilated upon Roman dolls and others — citing Persius, " *Veneri donato a virgine puppæ.*"

upon saving the half of this, and returning after five years with a moderate fortune. He did better, however — shortening his period of exile by nearly a twelve-month, and bringing back £30,000.

His sister (who later became Lady Trevelyan) went with him as the mistress of his Calcutta household ; and his affectionate and most tender relations with this, as well as with his younger sister, are beautifully set forth in the charming biography by his nephew, Otto Trevelyan. It is a biography that everybody should read ; and none can read it, I am sure, without coming to a kindlier estimate of its subject. The home-letters with which it abounds run over with affectionate playfulness. We are brought to no ugly *post mortem* in the book, and no opening of old sores. It is modest, courteous, discreet, and full.

Macaulay did monumental work in India upon the Penal Code. He also kept up there his voracious habits of reading and study. Listen for a moment to his story of this :

" During the last thirteen months I have read Eschylus, twice; Sophocles, twice; Euripides, once; Pindar, twice; Callimachus, Apollonius Rhodius, Theocritus, twice; Herodotus, Thucydides, almost all of Xenophon's works, almost all of Plato, Aristotle's *Politics*, and a good deal of his *Organon ;* the whole of Plutarch's Lives; half of Lucian; two or three books of Athenæus; Plautus, twice; Terence, twice; Lucretius, twice; Catullus, Propertius, Lucan, Statius, Silius Italicus, Livy, Velleius Paterculus, Sallust, Cæsar, and lastly, Cicero."

This is his classical list. Of his modern reading he does not tell ; yet he was plotting the *History of England,* and the bouncing balladry of the *Lays of Rome* was even then taking shape in the intervals of his study.

His father died while Macaulay was upon his voyage home from India — a father wholly unlike the son, in his rigidities and his Calvinistic asperities; but always venerated by him, and in the latter years of the old gentleman's life treated with a noble and beautiful generosity.

A short visit to Italy was made after the return from India ; and it was in Rome itself that he put some of the last touches to the Lays — staying the work until he could confirm by personal observation the relative sites of the bridge across the Tiber and the home of Horatius upon the Palatine.

You remember the words perhaps ; if not, 'twere well you should,—

> ' Alone stood brave Horatius,
>   But constant still in mind ;
> Thrice thirty thousand foes before,
>   And the broad flood behind.
> ' Down with him ! ' cried false Sextus,
>   With a smile on his pale face.
> ' Now yield thee,' cries Lars Porsena,
>   ' Now yield thee to our grace ! '
>
> Round turned he, as not deigning
>   Those craven ranks to see ;
> Nought spake he to Lars Porsena,
>   To Sextus nought spake he !
> But he saw on Palatinus
>   The white porch of his home ;
> And he spake to the noble river
>   That rolls by the towers of Rome.
>
> ' Oh, Tiber, father Tiber !
>   To whom the Romans pray,
> A Roman's life, a Roman's arms,
>   Take thou in charge this day ! '
> So he spake, and speaking sheathed
>   The good sword by his side,
> And, with his harness on his back,
>   Plunged headlong in the tide."

This does not sound like those verses of Shelley, which we lately encountered. Those went through the empyrean of song like Aurora's chariot of the morning, with cherubs, and garlands, and flashing torches. This, in the comparison, is like some well - appointed dump - cart, with sleek, well - groomed Percheron horses — up to their work, and accomplishing what they are set to do absolutely well.

It was not until 1842, a year or two after the Italian visit, that Macaulay ventured to publish that solitary book of his verse ; he very much doubted the wisdom of putting his literary reputation in peril by such overture in rhyme. It extorted, however, extravagant praise from that muscular critic Christopher North ; while the fastidious Hunt writes to him (begging a little money — as was his wont), and regretting that the book did not show more of the poetic aroma which breathes from the *Faeric Queenc.* But say what we may of its lack — there is no weakly maundering ; it is the work of a man full-grown, with all his wits active, and his vision clear, and who loved plain sirloins better than the fricandeaux and ragoûts of the artists.

There is also a scholarly handling, with high,

historic air blowing through — as if he liked his Homer better than his Spenser; his prosody is up to the rules; the longs and shorts are split to a hair's breadth — jingling and merry where the sense calls for it; and sober and resonant where meaning is weighty; flashing, too, where need is — with sword play and spear-heads that glitter and waver over marching men; but no-where — I think it must be said — the tremulous poetic *susurrus*, that falters, and touches, and de-tains by its mystic sounds — tempting one into dim border-lands where higher and more inspired singers find their way. Christabel is not of his school, nor the star-shaped shadow of Words-worth's Daisy.

Parliamentarian and Historian.

Meantime occasional papers from Macaulay's hand found their way into the pages of the great Northern *Review* — but by no means so many as the Whig managers could have wished; he had himself grown to think lightly of such work; the History was calling for his best powers, and there were parliamentary duties devolving upon him as member for Edinboro'.

I remember catching sight of him somewhere between 1844 and 1846 — in his place in the House of Commons, and of listening to his brilliant castigation of Sir. Robert Peel, in the matter, I think, of the Maynooth grant. He was well toward fifty then, but sturdy — with the firm tread of a man who could do his three or four leagues of walking — if need were ; beetle-browed ; his clothes ill-adjusted ; his neck bundled in a big swathing of cravat. There was silence when he rose ; there was nothing orator-like in his bearing ; rather awkward in his pose ; having scorn, too, as would seem, for any of the graces of elocution. But he was clear, emphatic, direct, with a great swift river of words all bearing toward definite aim. Tory critics used to say he wrote his speeches and committed them to memory. There was no need for that. Words tripped to his tongue as easily as to his pen. But there were no delicate modulations of voice ; no art of pantomime ; no conscious or unconscious assumption of graceful attitudes ; and when subject-matter enfevered and kindled him — as it did on that occasion — there was the hurry and the over-strained voice of extreme earnestness.

It was not very long after this that he met with a notable repulse from his old political supporters in Edinboro' that touched him grievously. But there were certain arts of the politician he could not, and would not learn; he could not truckle; he could not hobnob with clients who made vulgar claims upon him. He could not make domiciliary visits, to kiss the babies — whether of patrons, or of editors; he could not listen to twaddle from visiting committees, without breaking into a righteous wrath that hurt his chances. Edinboro', afterward, however, cleared the record, by giving him before his death a triumphant return to Parliament.

Meantime that wonderful History had been written, and its roll of magniloquent periods made echo in every quarter of the literary world. Its success was phenomenal. After the issue of its second couplet of volumes the publishers sent to the author a check for £20,000 on account. Such checks passing between publisher and author were

then uncommon ; and — without straining a point
— I think I may say they are now. With its Macaulay endorsement, it makes a unique autograph,
now in the possession of the Messrs. Longmans —
but destined to find place eventually among the
manuscript treasures of the British Museum.

The great history is a partisan history, but it is
the work of a bold and outspoken and manly partisan. The colors that he uses are intense and
glaring; but they are blended in the making of
his great panorama of King William's times, with
a marvellous art. We are told that he was an advocate and not a philosopher ; that he was a rhetorician and not a poet. We may grant all this,
and we may grant more — and yet I think we
shall continue to cherish his work. Men of
greater critical acumen and nicer exploration may
sap the grounds of some of his judgments ; cooler
writers, and those of more self-restraint, may draw
the fires by which his indignations are kindled ;
but it will be very long before the world will
cease to find high intellectual refreshment in the
crackle of his epigrams, in his artful deployment
of testimony, in his picturesque array of great

IV.—18

historic characters and in the roll of his sonorous periods.

Yet hé is the wrong man to copy; his exaltations make an unsafe model. He exaggerates — but he knows how to exaggerate. He paints a truth in colors that flow all round the truth, and enlarge it. Such outreach of rhetoric wants corresponding capacity of brain, and pen-strokes that never swerve or tremble. Smallish men should beware how they copy methods which want fulness of power and the besom of enthusiasm to fill out their compass. Homer can make all his seawaves iridescent and multitudinous—all his women high-bosomed or blue-eyed — and all his mountains sweep the skies : but *we* should be modest and simple.

It was not until Macaulay had done his last work upon the book (still incomplete) which he counted his monument, that he moved away from his bachelor quarters in the Albany (Piccadilly) and established himself at Holly Lodge, which, under the new name (he gave it) of Oirlie Lodge, may be found upon a winding lane in that labyrinth of city roads that lies between

Kensington Gardens and Holland House. There
was a bit of green lawn attached, which he came
to love in those last days of his; though he
had been without strong rural proclivities. Like
Gibbon, he never hunted, never fished, rarely
rode. But now and then — among the thorn-
trees reddening into bloom and the rhododendrons
bursting their buds, the May mornings were
" delicious" to him. He enjoyed, too, overmuch,
the modest hospitalities he could show in a home
of his own. There are joyfully turned notes — in
his journal or in his familiar letters — of " a goose
for Michaelmas," and of " a chine and oysters for
Christmas eve," and " excellent audit ale " on Lord
Mayor's day. There, too, at Holly Lodge, comes
to him in August, 1857, when he was very sad
about India (as all the world were), an offer of a
peerage. He accepts it, as he had accepted all the
good things of life — cheerily and squarely, and was
thenceforward Baron Macaulay of Rothley. He
appears from time to time on the benches of the
Upper House, but never spoke there. His speaking
days were over. A little unwonted fluttering of
the heart warned him that the end was not far off.

A visit to the English lakes and to Scotland in 1859 did not — as was hoped — give him access of strength. He was much disturbed, too (at this crisis), by the prospect of a long separation from his sister, Lady Trevelyan — whose husband had just now been appointed Governor of Madras. "This prolonged parting," he says, "this slow sipping of the vinegar and the gall is terrible!" And the parting came earlier than he thought, and easier ; for on a day of December in the same year he died in his library chair. His nephew and biographer had left him in the morning — sitting with his head bent forward on his chest — an attitude not unusual for him — in a languid and drowsy reverie. In the evening, a little before seven, Lady Trevelyan was summoned, and the biographer says :—" As we drove up to the porch of my uncle's house, the maids ran crying into the darkness to meet us ; and wo knew that all was over."

He was not an old man — only fifty-nine. The stone which marks his grave in Westminster Abbey is very near to the statue of Addison.

In estimating our indebtedness to Macaulay as

a historian — where his fame and execution were largest — we must remember that his method of close detail forbade wide outlook or grasp of long periods of time. If he had extended the same microscopic examination and dramatic exhibit of important personages to those succeeding reigns, which he originally intended to cover — coming down to the days of William IV.—he would have required fifty volumes; and if he had attempted, in the same spirit, a reach like that of Green or Hume, his rhetorical periods must have overflowed more than two hundred bulky quartos ! No ordinary man could read such ; and — thank Heaven ! — no extraordinary man could write so many.

Some Tory Critics.

Among those who sought with a delightsome pertinacity for flaws in the historic work of Macaulay, in his own time, was John Wilson Croker, to whom I have already alluded.* He was an older man than the historian ; Irish by birth, handsome, well-allied by marriage, plausible, fawning on the great (who were of *his* party) wear-

---

* See p. 116, *Ante.*

ing easily and boastfully his familiarity with Wellington, with Lansdowne and Cumberland, airing daintily his literary qualities at the tables of Holland or Peel; proud of his place in Parliament, where he loved to show a satiric grace of speech, and the curled lips of one used to more elegant encounters. In short, he was the very man to light up the blazing contempt of such another as Macaulay; more than all since Croker was identified with the worst form of Toryism, and the other always his political antagonist.

Such being the *animus* of the parties, one can imagine the delight of Croker in detecting a blunder of Macaulay, and the delight of Macaulay when he was able to pounce upon the blunders in Croker's edition of *Boswell's Johnson.* This was on many counts an excellent work and — with its emendations — holds its ground now; but I think the slaps, and the scourgings, and the derisive mockery which the critic dealt out to the self-poised and elegant Croker have made a highly appetizing *sauce piquante* for the book these many a year. For my own part, I never enjoy it half so much as when I think of Ma-

caulay's rod of discipline "starting the dust out
of the varlet's [editor's] jacket."

It is not a question if Croker deserved this ex-
coriation ; we are so taken up with the dexterity
and effectiveness with which the critical professor uses the surgeon's knife, that we watch the
operation, and the exceeding grace and ease with
which he lays bare nerve after nerve, without once
inquiring if the patient is really in need of such
heroic treatment.

The Croker Papers * — two ponderous volumes
of letters and diary which have been published in
these latter years — have good bits in them ; but
they are rare bits, to be dredged for out from
quagmires of rubbish. The papers are interesting,
furthermore, as showing how a cleverish man, with
considerable gifts of presence and of brain, with
his re-actionary Toryism dominant, and made a
fetich of, can still keep a good digestion and go in
a respectable fashion through a long life — back-
wards, instead of "face to the front."

In this connection it is difficult to keep out of

---

* *Memoirs and Correspondence*, 1885.

mind that other Toryish administrator of the
Quarterly bombardments of reform and of Liberal-
ists — I mean Lockhart (to whom reference has
already been made in the present volume), and
who, with all of Croker's personal gifts, added to
these a still larger scorn than that of his elder associate in the Quarterly conclaves, for those whose
social disabilities disqualified them for breathing
the rarefied air which circulated about Albemarle
Street and the courts of Mr. Murray.   Even Mr.
Lang in his apologetic but very interesting story
of Lockhart's life,* cannot forbear quiet repre-
hensive allusions to that critic's odious way of
making caustic allusion to " the social rank " of
political opponents ; although much of this he avers
" is said in wrath."   Yet it is an unworthy wrath,
always and everywhere, which runs in those direc-
tions.   Lockhart, though an acute critic, and a
very clever translator, was a supreme worshipper
of " conditions," rather than of qualities.   He
never forgave Americans for being Americans, and
never preter-mitted his wrathy exposition of their

---

* Lang's *Lockhart*, p. 42, vol. ii.

' low-lived antecedents ' socially. The baronetcy
of his father - in - law, Sir Walter Scott, was I
think, a perpetual and beneficent regalement to
him.

Two Gone-by Story Tellers.

Must it be said that the jolly story-teller of the
sea and of the sea-ports, who wrote for our uncles
and aunts, and elder brothers, the brisk, rollicking
tales about *Midshipman Easy*, and *Japhet in
Search of a Father*, is indeed gone by ?

His name was Frederick Marryat,* the son of a
well-to-do London gentleman, who had served the
little Borough of Sandwich as member of Parliament (and was also author of some verses and
political tractates), but who did not wean his boy
from an inborn love of the sea. To gratify this
love the boy had sundry adventurous escapades;
but when arrived at the mature age of fourteen, he
entered as midshipman in the Royal Navy — his

---

* Frederick Marryat, b. 1792; d. 1848; R. N., 1806;
Commander, 1815; resigned, 1830. *Frank Mildmay*, 1829;
Midshipman Easy, 1836; *Peter Simple*, 1837; *Jacob Faith-
ful*, 1838; *Life*, by his daughter, Florence, 1872.

first service, and a very active one, being with that brave and belligerent Lord Cochrane, who later won renown on the west coast of South America. Adventures of most hazardous and romantic qualities were not wanting under such an officer, all of which were stored in the retentive memory of the enthusiastic and observant midshipman, and thereafter, for years succeeding, were strewn with a free hand over his tales of the sea. These break a good many of the rules of rhetoric — and so do sailors; they have to do with the breakage of nearly all the commandments — and so do sailors. But they are breezy; they are always pushing forward; spars and sails are all ship-shape; and so are the sailors' oaths, and the rattle of the chain-cables, and the slatting of the gaskets, and the smell of the stews from the cook's galley.

There is also a liberal and *quasi* democratic coloring of the links and interludes of his novels. The trials of *Peter Simple* grow largely out of the cruel action of the British laws of primogeniture; nor does the jolly midshipman — grandson, or nephew — forego his satiric raps at my lord "Privilege." Yet Marryat shows no special admiration for such evolutions of the democratic problem as he encounters in America.*

Upon the whole, one finds no large or fine literary quality in his books; but the *fun* in them is positive, and catching — as our aunts and uncles used to find it; but it is the fun of the tap-room, and of the for'castle, rather than of the salon, or the library. For all this, scores and scores of excellent old people were shaking their sides — in the early part of this century — over the pages of Captain Marryat — in the days when other readers with sighs were bemoaning the loss of the " Great Magician's " power in the dreary story of *Count Robert of Paris,* or kindling into a new worship as they followed Ainsworth's † vivid narrative of Dick Turpin's daring gallop from London to York.

A nearer name to us, and one perhaps more familiar, is that of G. P. R. James,‡ an excellent,

---

* *Diary in America*, by Captain F. Marryat, 1839.

† William Harrison Ainsworth, b 1805; d. 1882. *Rookwood*, 1834 — chiefly notable for its wonderful description of Dick Turpin's ride — upon Black Bess — from London to York. *Tower of London*, 1840.

‡ G. P. R. James, b. 1801; d. 1860. *Richelieu* (first novel),

industrious man, who drove his trade of novel-making — as our engineers drive wells — with steam, and pistons, and borings, and everlasting clatter.

Yet,—is this sharp, irreverent mention, wholly fair to the old gentleman, upon whose confections, and pastries, so many of us have feasted in times past? What a delight it was — not only for young-sters, but for white-haired judges, and country lawyers — to listen for the jingle of the spurs, when one of Mr. James's swarthy knights—" with a grace induced by habits of martial exercise "— came dashing into old country quietudes, with his visor up; or, perhaps in "a Genoa bonnet of black velvet, round which his rich chestnut hair coiled in profusion"— making the welkin ring with his — "How now, Sir Villain!"

I caught sight of this great necromancer of "miniver furs," and mantua - making chivalry —

1829; *Darnley*, 1830; *One in a Thousand*, 1835; *Attila*, 1837. His books count far above a hundred in number: Lowndes (Bohn) gives over seventy titles of novels alone. What he might have done, with a modern type-writer at com-mand, it is painful to imagine.

in youngish days, in the city of New York —
where he was making a little over-ocean escape
from the multitudinous work that flowed from
him at home ; a well-preserved man, of scarce
fifty years, stout, erect, gray-haired, and with
countenance blooming with mild uses of mild
English ale — kindly, unctuous — showing no
signs of deep thoughtfulness or of harassing
toil.   I looked him over, in boyish way, for
traces of the court splendors I had gazed upon,
under his ministrations, but saw none ; nor
anything of the " manly beauty of features,
rendered scarcely less by a deep scar upon the
forehead," — nor " of the gray cloth doublets
slashed with purple ; " a stanch, honest, amiable,
well-dressed Englishman — that was all.

And yet, what delights he had conjured for us !
Shall we be ashamed to name them, or to confess
it all ?   Shall the modern show of new flowerets
of fiction, and of lilies — forced to the front in
January — make us forget utterly the old cinna-
mon roses, and the homely but fragrant pinks,
which once regaled and delighted us, in the April
and May of our age ?

What incomparable siestas those were, when, from between half-closed eyelids, we watched for the advent of the two horsemen — one in corselet of shining silver, inlaid with gold, and the other with hauberk of bright steel rings — slowly riding down the distant declivity, under the rays of a warm, red sunset! Then, there were abundance of gray castle - walls — ever so high, the ivy hanging deliciously about them ; and there were clanging chains of draw - bridges, that rattled when a good knight galloped over ; and there were stalwart gypsies lying under hedges, with charmingest of little ones with flaxen hair (who are not gypsies at all, but only stolen) ; and there is clash of arms ; and there are bad men, who get punched with spear heads — which is good for them ; and there are jolly old burghers who drink beer, and "troll songs" ; and assassins who lurk in the shadows of long corridors — where the moonbeams shine upon their daggers ; and there are dark - haired young women, who look out of casements and kiss their hands and wave white kerchiefs, — and somebody sees it in the convenient edge of the wood, and salutes in return, and steals away ; and the assassin escapes, and the gypsies are captured in the bush, and some bad king is killed, and an old parchment is found, and the stars come out, and the rivulet murmurs, and the good knight comes back ; and the dark tresses are at the casement, and she smiles, and the marriage bells ring, and they are happy. And the school bell (for supper) rings, and we are happy !

As I close this book with these last shadowy glimpses of story-tellers, who have told their pleasant tales, and have lived out their time, and gone to rest, I see lifting over that fair British horizon, where Victoria shows her queenly presence — the modest Mr. Pickwick, with his gaiters and bland expanse of figure ; Thackeray, too, with his stalwart form and spectacled eyes is peering out searchingly upon all he encounters ; the refined face of Ruskin is also in evidence, and his easy magniloquence is covering one phase of British art with new robes. A woman's Dantesque profile shows the striking qualities which are fairly mated by the striking passages in *Adam Bede* and *Daniel Deronda ;* one catches sight, too, of the shaggy, keen visage of the quarrel-loving Carlyle, and of those great twin-brethren of poesy — Browning and Tennyson — the Angelo and the Raphael of latter images in verse. Surely these make up a wonderful grouping of names — not unworthy of comparison with those others whom we found many generations ago, grouped around another great queen of England, who blazed in her royal court, and flaunted her silken robes, and — is gone.

INDEX.